BUILDING
HISTORY
SERIES

THE

WHITE

HOUSE

TITLES IN THE BUILDING HISTORY SERIES INCLUDE:

Alcatraz
The Eiffel Tower
The Great Wall of China
The Medieval Castle
The Medieval Cathedral
Mount Rushmore
The New York Subway System
The Palace of Versailles
The Panama Canal
The Parthenon of Ancient Greece
The Pyramids of Giza
The Roman Colosseum
Roman Roads and Aqueducts
Shakespeare's Globe
The Sistine Chapel
Stonehenge
The Titanic
The Transcontinental Railroad
The Viking Longship

BUILDING
HISTORY
SERIES

THE
WHITE
HOUSE

by Nathan Aaseng

Henry County Library System
Locust Grove Public Library
P.O. Box 240, 3918 Highway 42
Locust Grove, GA 30248

Lucent Books, Inc., San Diego, California

HENRY COUNTY LIBRARY SYSTEM
HAMPTON, LOCUST GROVE, McDONOUGH, STOCKBRIDGE

On Cover: The building of the White House, 1798 (left); The White House (top right); White House renovations under President Truman (bottom right).

Library of Congress Cataloging-in-Publication Data

Aaseng, Nathan.
   The White House / by Nathan Aaseng.
     p.   cm. — (Building history series)
   Includes bibliographical references and index.
   Summary: Discusses the history of the home of the United States president, including its location, design and construction, fire and rebuilding, renovations, and how it evolved into a modern residence.
   ISBN 1-56006-708-X (alk. paper)
   1. White House (Washington, D.C.)—Juvenile literature. 2. Washington (D.C.)—Buildings, structures, etc.—Juvenile literature. 3. Presidents—United States—Juvenile literature. [1. White House (Washington, D.C.) 2. Washington (D.C.)—Buildings, structures, etc. 3. Presidents.] I. Title. II. Series.
   F204.W5 A43 2001
   975.3—dc21

                                                    00-008238

Copyright 2001 by Lucent Books, Inc.
P.O. Box 289011, San Diego, California, 92198-9011

No part of this book may be reproduced or used in any other form or by any other means, electrical, mechanical, or otherwise, including, but not limited to, photocopy, recording, or any information storage and retrieval system, without prior written permission from the publisher.

Printed in the U.S.A.

CONTENTS

FOREWORD

Throughout history, as civilizations have evolved and prospered, each has produced unique buildings and architectural styles. Combining the need for both utility and artistic expression, a society's buildings, particularly its large-scale public structures, often reflect the individual character traits that distinguish it from other societies. In a very real sense, then, buildings express a society's values and unique characteristics in tangible form. As scholar Anita Abramovitz comments in her book, *People and Spaces,* "Our ways of living and thinking—our habits, needs, fear of enemies, aspirations, materialistic concerns, and religious beliefs—have influenced the kinds of spaces that we build and that later surround and include us."

That specific types and styles of structures constitute an outward expression of the spirit of an individual people or era can be seen in the diverse ways that various societies have built palaces, fortresses, tombs, churches, government buildings, sports arenas, public works, and other such monuments. The ancient Greeks, for instance, were a supremely rational people who originated Western philosophy and science, including the atomic theory and the realization that the earth is a sphere. Their public buildings, epitomized by Athens's magnificent Parthenon temple, were equally rational, emphasizing order, harmony, reason, and above all, restraint.

By contrast, the Romans, who conquered and absorbed the Greek lands, were a highly practical people preoccupied with acquiring and wielding power over others. The Romans greatly admired and readily copied elements of Greek architecture, but modified and adapted them to their own needs. "Roman genius was called into action by the enormous practical needs of a world empire," wrote historian Edith Hamilton. "Rome met them magnificently. Buildings tremendous, indomitable, amphitheaters where eighty thousand could watch a spectacle, baths where three thousand could bathe at the same time."

In medieval Europe, God heavily influenced and motivated the people, and religion permeated all aspects of society, molding people's worldviews and guiding their everyday actions. That spiritual mindset is reflected in the most important medieval structure—the Gothic cathedral—which, in a sense, was a model of heavenly cities. As scholar Anne Fremantle so ele-

6

gantly phrases it, the cathedrals were "harmonious elevations of stone and glass reaching up to heaven to seek and receive the light [of God]."

Our more secular modern age, in contrast, is driven by the realities of a global economy, advanced technology, and mass communications. Responding to the needs of international trade and the growth of cities housing millions of people, today's builders construct engineering marvels, among them towering skyscrapers of steel and glass, mammoth marine canals, and huge and elaborate rapid transit systems, all of which would have left their ancestors, even the Romans, awestruck.

In examining some of humanity's greatest edifices, Lucent Books' Building History series recognizes this close relationship between a society's historical character and its buildings. Each volume in the series begins with a historical sketch of the people who erected the edifice, exploring their major achievements as well as the beliefs, customs, and societal needs that dictated the variety, functions, and styles of their buildings. A detailed explanation of how the selected structure was conceived, designed, and built, to the extent that this information is known, makes up the majority of the volume.

Each volume in the Lucent Building History series also includes several special features that are useful tools for additional research. A chronology of important dates gives students an overview, at a glance, of the evolution and use of the structure described. Sidebars create a broader context by adding further details on some of the architects, engineers, and construction tools, materials, and methods that made each structure a reality, as well as the social, political, and/or religious leaders and movements that inspired its creation. Useful maps help the reader locate the nations, cities, streets, and individual structures mentioned in the text; and numerous diagrams and pictures illustrate tools and devices that bring to life various stages of construction. Finally, each volume contains two bibliographies, one for student research, the other listing works the author consulted in compiling the book.

Taken as a whole, these volumes, covering diverse ancient and modern structures, constitute not only a valuable research tool, but also a tribute to the human spirit, a fascinating exploration of the dreams, skills, ingenuity, and dogged determination of the great peoples who shaped history.

IMPORTANT DATES IN THE BUILDING OF THE WHITE HOUSE

July 16, 1790
Congress approves establishment of accommodations for the president at a new Federal City to be located on the Potomac River.

November 1, 1800
John Adams moves in.

1828
North portico added.

July 1792
James Hoban wins contest for design of Executive Mansion.

August 24–25, 1814
British troops set fire to President's House.

1817
Hoban completes rebuilding.

1790   **1800**   **1810**   **1820**   **1830**

October 13, 1792
Executive Mansion cornerstone laid.

1824
South portico added.

1791
George Washington appoints commissioners and hires Pierre L'Enfant to oversee development of Federal City; site of President's House chosen.

The White House circa 1860.

1873
First major refurbishing performed, during Grant administration.

1881
Tiffany refurbishing performed, during Arthur administration.

1909
Oval Office constructed.

The president's office about 1898.

1870   1890   1910   1930   1950   1970   1990

1902
Major reconstruction and enlargement during Theodore Roosevelt administration.

1927
Attic converted to third story.

May 1995
Pennsylvania Avenue closed due to security concerns.

1964
Congress establishes Committee for the Preservation of the White House.

1948–1952
Massive reconstruction of White House during Truman administration.

I INTRODUCTION

Had Pierre L'Enfant been allowed to finish his plans, the president of the United States would live in a mansion as colossal and magnificent as any castle found in the great capitals of Europe and Asia. The architect left no doubt as to the scope of his intention when he referred to his proposed masterpiece as the "Presidential Palace."

The building that finally emerged out of the swamplands of the brand-new city of Washington, D.C., at the turn of the nineteenth century was only a small fraction of the size that L'Enfant envisioned. Nor did it come close to L'Enfant's goal of an architectural wonder of the world. In the words of one historian, "As an architectural statement or an engineering accomplishment, the building is entirely unexceptional."[1] Furthermore, the people of the United States have never treated the residence at 1600 Pennsylvania Avenue with the pomp and reverence than L'Enfant had desired. Although the place was formally known as the Executive Mansion throughout its first century of existence, most people referred to it simply as the President's House. And John Adams, the first president to live in the building, had barely unpacked his bags before locals saddled it with a nickname as simple and plain as could be devised: the White House.

Because the nickname was easier to say than Executive Mansion or President's House, its use gradually became more common. During the term of James Madison, little more than a decade after the house was built, "White House" was commonly accepted in informal conversation. Eventually, by the 1860s, the name "White House" began appearing even in many public and government documents in reference to the president's home. The simplicity of the title appealed to Theodore Roosevelt, a man who hated bureaucracy and pretentiousness. One of his first acts on taking office in 1901 was to officially change the name of his new home to the White House. Today, the White House has become more than the name of a building; it is a symbol. Newspeople often use the term "White House" to refer to members of the executive branch of the federal government acting on behalf of the people of the United States.

A LIVING MONUMENT

Yet despite its common name and scaled-down design, the White House stands as one of the most important and fascinating structures ever built. It serves as a living monument—the first famous building constructed by the fledgling federal government of the United States. Most occupants of the White House have worked hard to protect its unique position in history. Despite numerous alterations and additions, the basic design of the building remains the same as when it was built two centuries ago.

The White House stands apart from the other government buildings of the world because it has had to perform three vastly different functions throughout its long life. It is simultaneously a public building, a government building, and a private residence.

As a public building, the White House is operated and maintained by the National Park Service, which took over the responsibility from the Army Corps of Engineers during Franklin Roosevelt's administration. It is the only residence of a prominent head of state that is regularly open to the public, free of charge.

The White House serves as the center of social activity for the executive branch of the government. Thousands of prominent individuals enter the White House as guests at dinners, receptions, and other formal functions that the president is expected to host.

President Theodore Roosevelt officially changed the name of the Executive Mansion to the White House.

Yet, in the midst of tourists and foreign dignitaries, the White House also provides a home for U.S. presidents and their families. The multiple function of the White House has created problems over the years. The presidents' families have had to resign themselves to the fact that, in some respects, the White House serves more as a hotel for temporary guests than as a private home. They have often struggled to carve out privacy for themselves, sometimes successfully, sometimes not.

For some families, living in the White House has been a wonderful experience. Julia Grant, who originally so detested the place that she begged her husband to let her stay at her I Street residence in Washington, found life at the President's Mansion to be far better than she had expected: "My life at the White House was like a bright and beautiful dream . . . and I wish it might have continued forever."[2] She was so distraught upon having to leave at the end of President Ulysses S. Grant's second term that she broke down in tears on her way out the door.

For others, the place has been a nightmare. Upon yielding the presidency to Abraham Lincoln, an exhausted James Buchanan

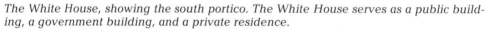

The White House, showing the south portico. The White House serves as a public building, a government building, and a private residence.

said, "If you are as happy, my dear sir, on entering this house as I am in leaving it and returning home, you are the happiest man in this country."[3]

But for the people of the United States, the White House is more than a residence, government building, or museum. It endures today as the symbol of the leader of the most powerful government on earth. John Adams, the first to occupy the building, recognized what the White House symbolized. On the night that he moved in, he wrote a letter to his wife in which he included a fervent wish. More than a century later, Franklin Roosevelt was moved to have that wish inscribed on the fireplace mantle of the State Room:

"I Pray Heaven to Bestow the Best of Blessings on THIS House and in ALL that shall hereafter Inhabit it. May none but Honest and Wise Men ever rule under this roof."[4]

THE FEDERAL CITY

The colonists who gained their independence from Great Britain in the American Revolution (1776–1783) struggled in their efforts to create a new nation. They realized they needed some sort of federal organization to hold the country together. Yet, having fought so hard to get out from under the oppression of one strong central government, many were reluctant to form another in its place.

Delegates from the thirteen colonies debated long and hard about what form the new government should take. Among the many issues they discussed was where the federal government should meet. Ever since the colonists first began openly planning their break from England in 1774, representatives from the separate colonies, or states as they have been known since the Revolution, had met in various cities. The site of these conventions rotated around the country, from Boston in the North, to Philadelphia and New York in the central part of the nation, to Charleston in the South. But most delegates recognized that, once established, the federal government would need to put down roots in a single spot. Permanent buildings would be needed to house the legislative body and officials of the executive branch.

NEEDED: A NEUTRAL SITE

In 1783 the temporary Congress met in Philadelphia, Pennsylvania. Most of those involved with forming national policy favored this city, the nation's largest, as the permanent home of the federal government.

But in June of that year, a large group of disgruntled soldiers marched to Philadelphia to confront federal officials. Many of them were desperately poor because the government had not made good on its promise to pay them for their years of service in the army during the Revolution. Since their home states did not have the money to pay them, they turned to the federal government in whose army they had fought. But though federal officials sympathized with the soldiers, they were helpless to act. The states' delegates to Congress had provided no means for the federal government to collect revenues and so they had no money to give.

As the soldiers' protests became more heated, federal officials pleaded with the governor of Pennsylvania to order the state militia to protect them. State officials, however, were reluctant to call out troops to confront its citizens on behalf of the unpopular federal government. Some of the soldiers then threatened to seize members of Congress until they got paid. Fearing for their safety, the federal officials quickly left town and reconvened in Princeton, New Jersey.

The incident demonstrated to many that the federal government should not be dependent on a particular state for protection.

THE UNITED STATES IN 1783

BRITISH NORTH AMERICA

TERRITORY GAINED BY TREATY OF PARIS

THE ORIGINAL THIRTEEN COLONIES

Mississippi River

Boston

New York

Philadelphia

Site of Washington, D.C.

Richmond

Charleston

Atlantic Ocean

SPANISH FLORIDA

If that state wished to oppose or control the federal government, it could shut it down or allow others to do so. Many people came to believe that the federal government should be set up some distance from large population centers to reduce the possibility of mobs trying to influence officials. This led to the idea of authorizing the federal government to buy land that would be set aside as a federal district, outside the rule of any state. A new federal city containing government offices and meeting halls could then be constructed in this district.

At this time, tensions were already growing between the populations of the northern colonies and the South. Delegates from each region maneuvered and schemed to have the new district located close to them. Some of the southern states began campaigning for a site along the Potomac River at the border of Virginia and Maryland. The land was completely undeveloped, yet the nearby rivers allowed for easy transportation and shipping. Representatives of other parts of the country, however, continued to campaign for their favorite cities to be designated as the nation's capital. Philadelphia and New York remained the top contenders for the honor.

Alexander Hamilton proposed Germantown, Pennsylvania, as the site for the nation's capital.

COMPROMISE

Alexander Hamilton, an astute New York politician with great influence among those who favored a strong federal government, finally gained the upper hand in this infighting. By the end of 1789, he had succeeded in lining up enough congressional votes to locate the nation's new capital in Germantown, Pennsylvania. The House of Representatives passed a bill authorizing this location for the new capital. The Senate, however, bogged down with a number of other issues, did not get around to approving the bill.

In the meantime a furious debate had arisen between the South and North over Hamilton's plan to have the federal government

WORKING TOGETHER

Had the debate over the location of the nation's capital occurred a decade later, the matter would not have been settled so peaceably. In 1790, however, the bitter political division between those who favored a strong central government (such as Washington, Adams, and Hamilton) and those who advocated limited government (Jefferson, Madison) had yet to break into the open. Jefferson was serving Washington's administration in the important role of secretary of state and was still on reasonably good terms with Hamilton.

In *The White House,* author Kenneth Leish details Jefferson's account of the day that he met an agitated Hamilton on the streets of Philadelphia. The two walked together for a half hour while Hamilton expressed his despair over the southern states' rejection of his plan for federal repayment of states' debts. Unless some way could be found soon to break the impasse, Hamilton feared that the nation would collapse into economic ruin.

Jefferson listened, and then agreed to see what he could do. The following day, he brought some influential members of Congress with him to a private dinner with Hamilton. In the course of their discussions, according to Jefferson,

> It was finally agreed that . . . the preservation of the Union and of the concord among the States was more important and that therefore it would be better that the vote of rejection should be rescinded, to the effect which some members should change their votes. But it was observed that this bill would be peculiarly bitter to the Southern States, and that some concomitant measure should be adopted to sweeten it a little to them.

The sweetening came in the form of locating the capital in a more southerly location.

Within a few years, a conversation between Jefferson and Hamilton such as the one that led to this compromise would have been impossible. The two became so bitterly opposed in their political philosophy that they could scarcely work together on any issue.

assume the war debts of each of the states. The governments of the northern states, which had still prepared no plan for paying the millions of dollars of outstanding debt, supported the plan. But the southern states had financed their part of the war effort by borrowing money from foreign countries. They had since repaid most of these debts. They were irate at the suggestion that their citizens, having acted responsibly in taking care of their debts, should be rewarded by having to contribute funds to repay the debts of the less responsible northern states.

Eventually, government leaders worked out a compromise. The southern states agreed to pass the repayment plan in exchange for a more southerly location for the capital. Legislation passed on July 16, 1790, establishing a commission that "Shall prior to the first Monday in December, in the year one thousand eight hundred, provide suitable buildings for the accommodation of Congress, and of the President, and for the public offices of the government of the United States."[5] Until that time, the federal government would continue to operate out of temporary quarters alternating between New York and Philadelphia. The Residence Bill authorized President George Washington to select a site on the Potomac River not to exceed ten square miles for the new Federal City.

OUT OF THE WILDERNESS

George Washington made the development of the Federal City and the President's House a major personal priority. He selected the sites for both, and according to William Seale, author of *The White House: An American Idea,* "In no endeavor did George Washington take a greater personal interest."[6] The site he chose for the city lay along the fork of the Potomac River and its east branch (later known as the Anacostia River). River access was crucial to the development of the district because it was the best means of transporting people and materials from one place to another.

Washington was very familiar with the area because it lay close to his own land in Virginia. According to a contemporary report, "Virtually all of it was undeveloped, with the land—some hilly, some more level—thickly covered with trees, crossed by several streams, and at places bordered by marshes."[7] Though the area was basically a wilderness, it lay near two small river towns that could accommodate shipping: the small tobacco-shipping port

An early view of Washington, D.C., facing west, with the Potomac River at left. Access to rivers for shipping was crucial to building the Federal City.

of Georgetown just a few miles to the west, and the growing port of Alexandria across the river.

Early in 1791, Washington appointed three commissioners to supervise the details of constructing the Federal City. At about the same time, he also hired an artist-engineer, Pierre Charles L'Enfant, whom he had known from their days in the Revolutionary army, to design the new district. By this time, most people were calling the new city Washington, in honor of the president. Washington, however, never referred to it as anything other than the Federal District, or District of Columbia.

L'Enfant was a dreamer who eagerly laid grand plans for what he hoped would be a city of unequaled majesty. He drew a rectangle of the prescribed ten square miles and placed it over a map of the land, with the Potomac River roughly in the center. The district cut into Maryland land on the northeast and Virginia land in the southwest.

L'Enfant's design of the city was heavily weighted toward artistic concerns as opposed to practical considerations. Using plans from several European cities as models, most particularly the elegant French city of Versailles, he put forth a plan for a city crisscrossed by wide diagonal boulevards. At various places in the city, he put in squares, circles, and triangular plots of land for parks, monuments, gardens, and fountains.

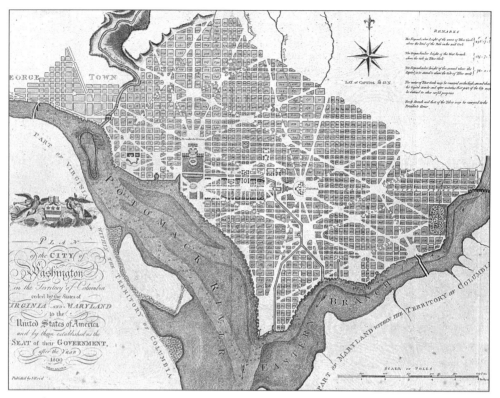

A plan of the Federal District from about 1800 shows the new city crisscrossed by L'Enfant's diagonal streets.

The key restriction on his design was that, by a decree of Congress, all the buildings had to be located on the Maryland side of the river. This arrangement conformed to the terms of a deal made to satisfy those who complained that Virginia (home of Washington, Thomas Jefferson, James Madison, and other prominent statesmen) was gaining too much influence among the states.

L'Enfant's geometrical layout of the city was based on a vision in his head that did not always fit the actual terrain. It was the job of Major Andrew Ellicot to survey the land and determine exactly how L'Enfant's plan could be adapted to the terrain. The survey was completed in the spring of 1791; L'Enfant presented to Washington his plan for the Federal District on June 22 of that year.

Although he delegated the details to others, Washington personally made or approved all the major decisions involving the new district. Even while L'Enfant was laying plans for the city, Washington scouted the area, seeking promising locations for the proposed President's House. One spot in particular caught his eye. There was a ridge overlooking a sluggish stream that L'Enfant called the Tiber River but which local hunters knew as Goose Creek because of the abundance of waterfowl in the area. Washington saw that a house facing south on that ridge would command a beautiful view of the Potomac River for about ten miles.

Taking Washington's advice, L'Enfant made a preliminary choice of a site for what he envisioned as the President's Mansion

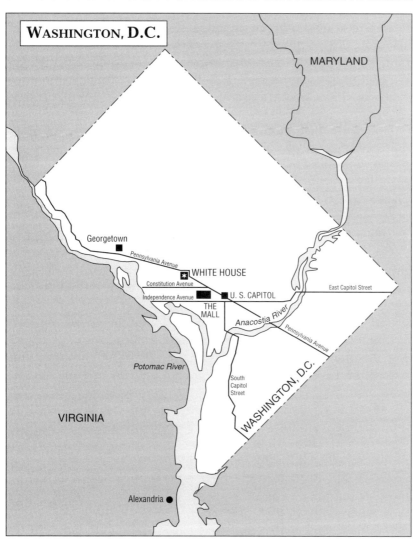

on that ridge, as well as a site for the Federal House (eventually known as the Capitol) on a second ridge, Jenkins Hill, about a mile to the east. He laid plans for a vast park or mall between the two buildings.

On June 28, L'Enfant toured the area with Washington and Ellicot to get final approval of the location of the federal buildings. Washington liked L'Enfant's plan, but made a slight adjustment in the site of the President's Mansion, moving it to an eighty-acre plot slightly to the west.

L'ENFANT KINDLES CONTROVERSY

President Washington knew that Jefferson and many others had a much less grandiose concept of what the capital should be than he did. He preferred to entrust the design of the city and the buildings completely to L'Enfant, who shared Washington's vision of a spectacular federal city that would command the respect of the nations of the world.

In keeping with that vision, the palace that L'Enfant planned for the president was enormous in scale. However, while Washington approved the general dimensions of the project, even he did not know the specifics of the plan. L'Enfant apparently made no sketches or drawings of the house but was working from an idea in his head.

Washington assumed L'Enfant was proceeding on the project during 1791. He was disturbed when weeks passed with no sign of progress. In September 1791, the impatient district commissioners, supported by Secretary of State Thomas Jefferson, decided to advertise for contestants to submit their plans for the President's House. Washington, however, withheld his approval of their idea. He was still counting on L'Enfant to come through. The designer finally began excavating the site in autumn, but even then no one knew exactly what he had in mind for this great palace.

Meanwhile, L'Enfant was running into problems with the three district commissioners. Headstrong and arrogant, he often went ahead with some aspect of development without the proper authorization. He refused to recognize the commissioners' authority or to accept criticism or suggestions from anyone but Washington. He assumed that Congress believed, as he and Washington did, in the need for an impressive federal city with magnificent buildings, and that Congress would provide the

BANNEKER AND THE FOUNDING OF THE CAPITAL

One of the key players in the design of Washington, D.C., was Benjamin Banneker, the first well-known black intellectual in the United States. Banneker was born on November 9, 1731, in Ellicott's Mills, Maryland, the son of a freed black slave. At a time when many people thought blacks incapable of academic success, he learned to read from his mother and grandmother. With that knowledge he taught himself a vast array of subjects from mathematics to astronomy, while earning a living farming tobacco.

His neighbors, the Ellicotts, were a Quaker family that did not share the prevailing prejudices against blacks. Impressed by Banneker's intelligence and inventive mind, George Ellicott recruited him to help out on several surveying projects. When Andrew Ellicott was awarded the job of surveying the new federal district, his cousin George recommended he hire Banneker as an assistant.

Andrew did so, and thus began what Banneker called the greatest adventure of his life. He and Ellicott arose well before dawn each day so they could begin surveying the district by sunrise. They worked until the sun set every day, seven days a week, until the massive job of siting and laying out L'Enfant's ambitious plan was complete. Despite the grueling pace, Banneker missed only one day of work. His detailed notes, complex calculations, and use of astronomical tools for marking base points proved invaluable in the design of the city.

The title page of an almanac published by Banneker.

funding to achieve it. His extravagant ideas reflected his belief that money was no object.

Unfortunately, the federal government was more starved for cash than ever. By assuming the war debts of the states, it had put itself deeply into debt, without much income to whittle down that debt. Initial funding for the federal projects had come from Maryland and Virginia, in appreciation for having the city located within their borders. But the federal government had counted on the sale of lots to private investors for the bulk of the development funds. Sales proved disappointing, mainly because the government failed to provide improvements such as good roads that would attract investors.

The district commissioners repeatedly tried to scale back L'Enfant's plans to a more realistic level, but he ignored them. The last straw came when L'Enfant found that one of the few land speculators to build in the federal district had erected a house in the way of one of L'Enfant's proposed avenues. Without consulting anyone, L'Enfant had the house torn down. The owner turned out to be Daniel Carroll, who was not only the largest property owner in the Federal District but also the uncle of one of the district commissioners. Carroll raised a storm of protest.

As much as he admired L'Enfant, Washington could not let him so blatantly thumb his nose at the commissioners whom he himself had appointed. On February 27, 1792, he dismissed L'Enfant from his duties. Infuriated, L'Enfant left the district, leaving behind nothing but a large hole in the ground to indicate what he had planned for the President's Mansion.

Designing the President's House

When L'Enfant's vision suddenly vanished from the scene, Washington had little choice but to agree to Jefferson's suggestion of a contest to attract designs for both the President's House and the Federal House. Within a month of L'Enfant's dismissal, the district commissioners—David Stuart, Daniel Carroll, and William Johnson—placed advertisements for the President's Mansion contest in the Philadelphia, Boston, Baltimore, Charleston, and Richmond newspapers. The ads laid out the specific requirements for the building and promised the winner an award of $500, a gold medal, and employment as a supervisor in the project.

"Pile of Trash"

The President's Mansion contest was a shot in the dark. There was not a single school of architecture in the United States at that time. The only architects and builders in the nation were a small number of immigrants educated in Europe and others who were self-taught. Therefore, the pool of professionals available to submit a plan was tiny.

Many of these experts either were too busy to submit a proposal or had no enthusiasm for the project. The difficulties caused by the rift with L'Enfant and the lack of interest among private businesspeople in developing the Federal District encouraged opponents of the project to step up their opposition. Fearful that a federal government given its own city would gain too much power and take control from the states, they called for the abandonment of the whole scheme. Influential people in Philadelphia and New York began drawing plans for elaborate President's Houses in their respective cities in hopes of winning approval as the nation's capital. John McComb, one of the most respected architects in the nation, designed a president's home in New York and declined to take part in the contest sponsored by the federal district commissioners.

Thomas Jefferson anonymously submitted a design for the President's Mansion.

By early June, three months after the contest was announced and barely a month from the deadline, the commissioners had received only two entries. Awareness of the lack of response prompted a flurry of entries from people who had neither training nor experience in designing a building on such a large scale as Washington proposed. One contemporary, George Hadfield, called the entries "the pile of trash presented as designs."[8] Washington, who examined the entries before sending them on to the commissioners, was appalled. He complained to Jefferson, "If none more elegant than these should appear . . . the exhibit will be a dull one indeed."[9] The lackluster quality of the entries persuaded Jefferson to anonymously submit a design of his own.

ENTER JAMES HOBAN

The builder who took the contest most seriously was James Hoban of South Carolina. Hoban had been educated in architectural studies in his native Ireland. After immigrating to the United States, he had risen quickly in the ranks of southern builders. Admiration for his work in designing their state capitol, completed in 1787, led South Carolina officials to introduce him to George Washington when the president visited Charleston in 1791.

Hoban thought carefully about the contest, and methodically went about giving himself the best chance of winning. He traveled to Philadelphia to meet with President Washington, carrying letters of recommendation from South Carolina officials. Instead of simply sitting down and designing his own version of the President's Mansion, Hoban asked Washington for his vision.

Although he had been content to give L'Enfant a free hand in his designs, Washington held some very definite ideas about the President's House. He was quite knowledgeable on the subject of architecture. He had designed a church built near his home and had planned and carried out a series of striking additions to his Mount Vernon residence. A Polish visitor to Mount Vernon wrote, "The General has never left America, but when one sees his house and his garden it seems as if he had copied the best samples of the grand old homesteads in Europe."[10]

Casting a critical eye on the house that would stand as a symbol to the nation and compete with the great halls of Europe,

JAMES HOBAN: WHITE HOUSE DESIGNER

James Hoban was born in Callan, Ireland, in 1762. He received his education in architecture at the Dublin Society Architectural School, where he won a medal for excellence in drawing. While living in Dublin, he had the opportunity to work on some of the most admired buildings in the world.

Unfortunately, architects were not in high demand at the time and Hoban could not make much money at his profession in Ireland. At the end of the American Revolution, he immigrated to the United States. After starting out in Philadelphia, he settled in the warmer climate of Charleston, South Carolina. There he made a good living designing and building plantation houses.

Despite having no experience in creating large public buildings, he offered to design and build South Carolina's capitol building. Since no one else in the area had any experience, he won the job, as his work was widely admired. That experience led him to enter the President's House contest.

Once Hoban arrived in the new Federal District, he found the opportunities for work almost limitless. He worked for nine years on the President's House, and then put in another four years at the Capitol. Eventually, he supervised the building of the Treasury and War Department Buildings, constructed two hotels, and built numerous private homes.

Always active in promoting the growth of the city he helped build, Hoban was elected to the first Washington, D.C., city council, and remained a councilman for the rest of his life.

THE ONLY NONRESIDENT PRESIDENT

One of the greatest ironies of the White House is that the person most responsible for its existence is the only president in history who never set foot in it. George Washington spent most of his presidency in a rented house in Philadelphia owned by financier Robert Morris.

The first U.S. president, George Washington.

Washington was determined to see the Federal City and the President's House become realities, and it took all of his considerable persuasiveness and popularity to make it happen. His scheme for financing the new Federal City was largely a disaster that nearly sank the whole plan. Washington, however, refused to be discouraged by the Federal City's struggles or swayed by Philadelphia's campaign to win acceptance as the nation's capital. His unwavering support of the Federal City and the President's House carried it through the worst times. Washington's second term of office ended in 1797, while the president's house was under construction. He died on December 14, 1799, less than a year before one of the crown jewels of his administration was put into use.

Washington cited "size, form, and elegance"[11] as the keys to its design. Foremost in his mind was the need to look to the future. In other words, while the United States was presently a relatively small and powerless nation, Washington dreamed that it would one day rank among the greatest nations of the world, and that its architecture should take that into account. He worried that a house simply fitting the requirements of the present chief executive would quickly be outgrown as the nation grew. Yet he realized a colossal mansion with empty rooms built to meet potential future needs would look silly and wasteful. "It was always my idea," Washington once wrote, "that the building should be so arranged that only a part of it should be erected for the present, and that upon such a plan as to make the part so erected an entire building and to admit of an addition in the future as circumstances might render proper, without hurting but rather adding to the beauty and magnificence of the whole." [12]

Hoban further aided his cause by being the only contest entrant to take the time to consult with the three commissioners. These officials appreciated Hoban's thoroughness, and noted in a report, "Mr. Hoban applies himself closely to a Draft of the President's House. He has made a very favorable Impression on us." [13]

Hoban then went to the actual building site with his drawing instruments. Taking in the lay of the land and remembering all of Washington's suggestions, he began to draw plans on the spot.

By the competition deadline of July 16, 1792, the commissioners had received seven proposals worthy of consideration from designers in five states. Two days later, Washington visited the commissioners in Georgetown to judge the entries. The winner was Hoban, whose three-story, boxlike structure included the important feature of wings that could be expanded almost indefinitely without hurting the overall appearance of the house.

The commissioners also were so impressed with the entry of John Collins of Virginia that they decided to honor him

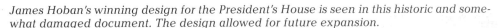

James Hoban's winning design for the President's House is seen in this historic and somewhat damaged document. The design allowed for future expansion.

with a prize of $150. The final design of the President's Mansion also paid a compliment to each contestant by incorporating some element of all submitted designs. For example, the size and shape of the building ended up being closer to the plans of Jacob Small of Maryland than to those of Hoban. James Diamond, also of Maryland, proposed arched, covered passageways leading to wings that could be added to either side of the main building. This is exactly what Jefferson and others eventually used to expand the building to its present form.

THE DESIGN

According to Ryan and Guiness in *The White House: An Architectural History,* "Hoban's composition was utterly new to America; no other building like it existed in the colonies of the early republic."[14] Even so, Hoban never pretended that his design for the President's House was entirely original. Architects of the time commonly chose their designs from one of many illustrated books on architecture. Given the extremely tight deadline imposed by the commissioners for the contest, putting together a new design from scratch on such a large scale would have been next to impossible.

There is some debate over exactly what model or models Hoban used for his design. Some historians suggest that Hoban was strongly influenced by a design illustrated in a basic reference book on architecture by James Gibbs, published in 1728.

Ryan and Guiness, however, disagree.They point out that, despite some similarities between the President's House and the illustration, there is no evidence to link the two. Contrary to Hoban's original design, the cited illustration is not even a three-story building.

Historians note that a variety of people familiar with Hoban and the construction of the President's House all refer to a house built for the Irish duke of Leinster as the inspiration for Hoban's design. The general plan of the entrance elevation and the first floor, which includes most of the rooms best known to the public, is virtually identical to that of Leinster. Hoban's original plan called for a building of dimensions almost identical to those of Leinster.

Had the President's House been nothing more than a copy of the Leinster house, however, neither Washington nor Jefferson would have been pleased. They both insisted that it have some stamp of American independence. Hoban's design met that standard with an exterior and upper floor plan that was completely of his own invention.

JEFFERSON AND THE DESIGN NOT CHOSEN

Of all the U.S. presidents, Thomas Jefferson was by far the most well educated in the field of architecture. Marshall Davidson, in *The American Heritage History of Notable American Houses,* quotes him as writing, "Architecture is my delight, and putting up, and pulling down one of my favorite amusements." His lifelong fascination with the subject began with his constant tinkering with his home, Monticello. During his travels to Europe on government business, he always took time to study the best architectural designs in whatever land he was visiting. When he returned home, he put into practice what he had learned. After viewing Jefferson's estate, a French nobleman enthused, "Thomas Jefferson is the first American who has consulted the Fine arts to learn how to shelter himself from the weather."

Jefferson's overall influence on American architecture was significant. As governor of Virginia, he redesigned the state capitol. Later in life, he planned the buildings for the University of Virginia. According to Davidson, Jefferson "was largely responsible for guiding the interest of the American people straight back to the building and culture of ancient Greece and Rome."

Jefferson tried to stamp that influence on the President's Mansion as well. He frequently made suggestions to Washington, promoting his idea of using Roman temples as a model. When the president proved to be less than enthusiastic about his plans, he submitted his own design to the building competition under the alias AZ. Had Jefferson's plan been adopted, the President's Mansion would have been far more flamboyant than that which was built. Among his proposals was a central dome made of alternating segments of solid structure and glass.

The major flaw in Jefferson's plan was that he failed to take into account Washington's requirement that the building be easily extended. When he failed to win the contest, Jefferson kept his involvement a secret. None of his contemporaries ever knew the identity of the mysterious AZ. Not until 1915, when a historian found an identical preliminary drawing of the AZ design among Jefferson's collection of private papers, was the secret revealed.

LEINSTER

Leinster was built in 1745 for an Irish gentleman who had the highest rank of any nobleman in the land. The house, which was an example of Greek architecture, was the largest townhouse in Ireland. The design came from an immigrant German civil engineer named James Castle.

Having studied architecture in Ireland, Hoban would have been quite familiar with Leinster. Historians suspect he may have had views of the building on hand to show Washington to gain approval before going ahead with his design.

The duke of Leinster was highly regarded for his support of projects that benefited the entire community. Washington himself was an admirer, and some historians suspect that this may have made the president especially favorable to a design patterned after the duke's house.

DESIGN TINKERING

The Hoban design that won the competition was not the final version that arose on the hill overlooking the Potomac. The question of size repeatedly came up for discussion. The President's House, as originally proposed by Hoban, would be the largest individual residence in the United States. Yet Washington, envisioning the nation grown to a respected world power, wondered if such a building was impressive enough to stand as a symbol of the nation. Before heading back to the temporary capital of Philadelphia, he insisted that Hoban enlarge it by one-fifth. Jefferson, who was skeptical of lavish government trappings, questioned whether this was necessary. He once described the President's House as "big enough for two emperors, one Pope, and the grand lama." [15]

However, even with the increase ordered by Washington, the President's House was barely one-quarter the size of the great palace that L'Enfant had been preparing. L'Enfant's crew had already dug out an enormous foundation that would swallow up the latest version. The commissioners had to reexamine their choice of site. Did they want to put the house in the middle of the huge pit, or would a smaller house be better situated off to one side or the other? When the commissioners were unable to come to an agreement on the issue, they called in Washington. The president visited the site and personally drove stakes into the ground at the northern extreme of L'Enfant's rectangle to mark the position of the house.

With the final design in hand, Washington pushed the project along. Already nearly three years of the ten provided by Congress for building the President's House had expired and there was nothing to show for that time but an overlarge hole. After his experiences entrusting the project to the temperamental L'Enfant, Washington wanted a construction supervisor he could trust. Hoban was the logical choice. He knew his own design intimately and was experienced in supervising construction of a large public building. But equally as important, he had been reliable and he had bent over backward to accommodate Washington's ideas.

Hoban redug the foundation to the correct dimensions and laid a firm bed of stones, gravel, wood, and sand on which the building would be erected. Following a festive parade, the cornerstone for the President's House was laid on October 13, 1792, the three hun-

James Hoban, architect of the White House and the Capitol.

dredth anniversary of Columbus's first voyage to the Americas. With the onset of winter, little else could be done until the following year.

ANOTHER DESIGN CHANGE

Almost immediately, Hoban ran into a problem that required yet another revision of his design. In keeping with his vision of a majestic house worthy of the world's respect, President Washington had insisted that the building be entirely faced with stone, including intricate, ornate carvings. The problem was that there was no established stone industry anywhere near the Federal District. National pride ruled out importing stone from England, the best source of dressed (trimmed and smoothed) stone. No one in the government wanted to be dependent on the country from whom they had just won their independence. Stone was available in some of the larger U.S. cities, but poor trans-portation over distance made that potential source impractical.

That left only the Aquia Creek quarry forty miles to the south, near Washington's home of Mount Vernon, as a possible source of stone. But the quarry was small, used mainly for sup-plying tombstones. As plans for both the President's House and the Capitol progressed, it quickly became clear that the quarry did not contain enough stone for both projects.

Meanwhile, the new nation continued to struggle with in-come shortages. The prices the government was negotiating on the land sales that were supposed to finance construction were disappointing. Congress made it clear that it would not come up with any extra funds for what some viewed as an extravagant palace, despite the severe curtailing of L'Enfant's plans. As time went on, the members of Congress grew more interested in the work on its own Capitol than on the President's House. For both financial constraints and lack of suitable stone, the commission-ers recommended replacing the stone on the President's House with more conventional and inexpensive brick.

Hoban, however, knew better than to make such a drastic change without the president's consent. Informed of the commis-sioners' concerns, Washington held fast to his preference for stone. His solution to the problem was a reluctant admission that they would have to scale down the house. He sent Hoban back to the drawing board to take out the raised lower floor that would have made the building three stories high. This cost-saving and stone-saving measure reduced the structure to two stories plus a basement. Washington also conceded the reality that they could not afford the splendid marble floor that had been planned, and instead would have to use wood.

The stone problem set a pattern for Hoban's construction procedure. He remained in frequent contact with Washington. Whenever the commissioners or anyone else threatened to in-terfere with his plans, he took up the matter with the president, who frequently intervened on his behalf.

BUILDING THE PRESIDENT'S HOUSE

During the construction, Hoban constantly suffered a shortage of skilled laborers. There were few such workers in the colonial United States to begin with, and the problem was magnified by the location of the federal capital. The two states that surrounded it, Virginia and Maryland, depended heavily on slave labor. Most tradesmen laborers did not like to work in areas where slavery existed because they could not compete with workers who were paid little or nothing, so most of them settled in the North.

Neither Hoban nor the commissioners had an organized plan for recruiting skilled workers from northern cities. For the most part, they depended on word of mouth to reach those tradesmen and attract them to the project.

Among these was Collen Williamson, a sixty-five-year-old master mason from the village of Dyke in northeastern Scotland who had recently settled in New York. Williamson's cousin happened to own a tavern where the district commissioners often met to discuss their project. After hearing them complain about the difficulty of finding expert stoneworkers, he contacted Williamson, who presented himself to the commissioners and was hired in April 1792.

Williamson's first responsibility was to develop and expand the tiny quarry at Aquia Creek. The commissioners contracted to supply him with "twenty-five able-bodied Negro men slaves"[16] to do the manual labor. First, the men had to clear the vegetation to expose new stone surfaces. Then, using hand-picks, they began cutting out blocks of stone. According to Lee H. Nelson in *White House Stone Carving,*

> The operation required considerable judgment and experience. To split the stone away, a number of iron wedges were placed in grooves about one foot apart

and systematically and uniformly driven into the grooves, splitting the large block into the desired size. It was a very slow process, involving a tremendous amount of physical labor.[17]

Marks made by masons in the original sandstone.

The blocks were then pulled out with cranes and pulleys to a level spot, where the workers cut them to the exact dimensions required. This stone was then hauled on wooden sleds to ships, each of which could carry thirty tons of stone. Because of the shallowness of the creek, the ships could be loaded only at high tide.

STONE LAYERS AND STONE CARVERS

By April 1793, enough stone had been quarried and prepared to begin construction. Williamson then moved on to his second responsibility, supervising the laying of the stone. Working with blocks of three hundred to three thousand pounds, the workers lifted and precisely fitted each into place. Williamson's crews cut, hauled, and laid 11 million tons of stone in the foundation walls. Hoban further estimated that one-eighth of the stones hauled from Aquia Creek were not usable and had to be discarded. The workers were fortunate that L'Enfant's ideas had been scaled back; his vision originally called for twice as much stone as was ultimately used.

Once the basic stonework was finished, in August 1794, a call went out for stone carvers who could create the artistic designs that Washington wanted. The commissioners asked Philadelphia merchant George Waller to recruit such artisans during a business trip to London. Finding no takers there, he moved on to Edinburgh, Scotland, whose stoneworkers were widely regarded as some of the world's best. At the time of the President's House construction, Great Britain had placed a moratorium, or ban, on building projects in the country because of the expense of waging war against France. Unable to find work in their native land, seven members of a masonic lodge in Edinburgh agreed to take on the task.

CUSTOM-MADE CARVING

These workers created a new problem, however. According to Nelson, "Unlike other tradesmen at the White House, such as carpenters, the Scotsmen objected to using slaves as hired help to assist them."[18] Desperate for workers, the government backed down and allowed them to take on white apprentices.

None of the thousands of carvings that were installed could be mass produced. Each carver put his own mark on every scroll, rose, leaf, flower, medallion, and ribbon that he created. Under the direction of chief stonemaster Williamson, the walls of the building began to rise, decorated by some of the finest and most elaborate carvings to appear on the American continent.

Williamson, however, did not last long in this final task. For while Hoban kept on good terms with his superiors, the same was not true of Williamson. A master craftsman with many years of experience, Williamson was used to being in complete control of the design and execution of projects. Hoban, on the other hand, was not about to trust any portion of this important project to any underling, and he insisted on approving all of the stonework designs in advance. Williamson resented this restriction and hard feelings between the two grew increasingly bitter. By 1795, the two

Intricate stonework crowns the north front entrance.

quarreled so frequently that Hoban dismissed Williamson from the project.

The chief stonemaster's departure left a leadership void among the stonemasons. Hoban never was able to find a replacement for Williamson. Thus, the stonemasons worked largely without supervision from 1795 until the completion of the stonework in 1798.

WHY THE PRESIDENT'S HOUSE BECAME WHITE

The stone from the Aquia Creek quarry was of a type called arkose sandstone. This soft, highly porous material was well suited for the type of ornate building Washington had in mind because it was easy to cut and carve. The disadvantage of the stone was that it did not weather well; it would quickly erode unless it was immediately sealed. The Scottish stonecutters had to brush each section of wall with a sealer, forcing the liquid into every crack and joint, as soon as it was complete.

The sealer they used was a dense, lime-based whitewash that gave the building its characteristic color. The combination of salt, ground rice, glue, water, and lime adhered so tightly to the stone that later renovators found it almost impossible to remove. Over the years, the exterior has been repainted several dozens of times, always white.

OTHER TRADESMEN

Seale notes that "of the trades other than stone masonry we know very little, for the original work is gone."[19] Records do indicate that among the first tradesmen to arrive, in the fall of 1793, were brickmaster Jeremiah Kale and his crew. Although Washington insisted on stone for the exterior, a large number of bricks were needed for supporting structures and the interior walls. During the working seasons from 1793 until October 1797, Kale kept two kilns fired up almost constantly, baking the necessary bricks. By the end of 1793, his bricklayers were able to complete work on the basement walls.

Eventually, the bricklayers and stonemasons were joined by two teams of carpenters. Peter Lennox supervised the group that worked on the large framing timbers that supported the roof and walls. Later, Joseph Middleton and his crew joined the workforce to perform smaller tasks such as building interior doors and window sashes.

The work site at times resembled an army camp. During the working season it was swarming with well over a hundred workers and dotted with shacks where workers were quartered. The grounds were littered with piles of materials. Supervisors called out the roll first thing in the morning, military style. A system of fines punished unacceptable behavior, such as reporting for work late, showing up drunk, or refusing to work on the highest part of the house. The work progressed steadily, six days a week, with only Sunday as a day of rest. Every year in the late autumn, the crews packed the walls and stone in sand and straw to protect them from the winter elements and abandoned the site until spring.

DIFFICULTIES

For the most part, the work progressed close to schedule, with Hoban in firm control of the entire operation. The only delays were largely a result of his prudent policy of consulting Washington and the commissioners on all major decisions. Occasionally, important matters of state arose that consumed the full attention of Washington's administration. When Jefferson's resignation as secretary of state forced a reorganization of the president's government, when

George Washington (left) and James Hoban (pointing) observe the progress of the President's Mansion in 1798.

tensions between the United States and Great Britain threatened to provoke a war, and when farmers in Massachusetts organized a brief armed revolt in opposition to tax policy, the President's House construction took a back seat.

THE PRESIDENT'S MANSION TAKES SHAPE

Gradually, the President's Mansion began to rise above the empty streets of the undeveloped Federal City. By November 1796, the framework for the interior walls was in place. The following year, the stone carvers completed their work on the exterior of the house. In October 1798, workers installed a ponderous slate roof over the building.

This finished the exterior of the grandest house ever built in the United States up to that time. The building featured strikingly different entrances on the north and south faces. The south front was distinguished by a lofty, three-story bay. Four attached Ionic columns gave the north entrance the stately elegance of an ancient Greek temple. The east and west sides of the building had no such striking features—they were basically the twin wings that Washington had wanted that could be extended in the future to enlarge the house without ruining its attractive proportions.

With the deadline for the government move to Washington approaching, workers picked up the pace. Plasterer Hugh Densley began finishing the interior walls in April 1799. He had fires kept burning in all thirty-nine of the house's fireplaces to speed the drying of the plaster.

Despite the best efforts of the workers, the building was nowhere near completion when President John Adams arrived, as scheduled, on November 1, 1800. There was a gaping hole in the main part of the building where the staircase was to be installed. None of the rooms were finished and the walls of several still lacked plaster.

The new city of Washington was still basically a large clearing cut out of the wilderness. When the federal government moved its entire headquarters there, fewer than five hundred houses had been built in the entire district. First Lady Abigail Adams, journeying a short way from Baltimore, Maryland, to join her husband, got lost trying to find the place. When she arrived at her new home, she had to make do with an alarming lack of facilities in a building that was meant to inspire pride in Americans. Only six of the rooms were in usable condition. The Adamses had to make do with old furniture brought down from the Philadelphia house that Washington had rented during his term. Mrs. Adams was forced to use the huge unfinished East Room, meant for elegant public gatherings, for hanging her laundry.

JEFFERSON AND LATROBE FINISH UP

Adams was frustrated by lack of money in his attempts to finish construction of the President's House. His plans were further stymied by the U.S. voters, who stunned him by rejecting his reelection bid in 1800. Only a few months after his family had moved in, Adams found himself giving up the keys to the mansion to his bitter rival, Thomas Jefferson.

John Adams completed his term in the unfinished President's House.

Jefferson was primarily occupied with the construction of the Capitol during the early years of his administration and had little time or money to spend on the President's House. Nonetheless, he never in his life lived in a house without adapting it to his own ideas, and the President's House was no exception. He took the opportunity that he had earlier been denied to help shape the nation's most famous residence.

In Jefferson's view, the main portion of the dwelling was too large and pretentious. Although there was little he could do at this point to convert the place into the kind of stately Roman temple that he had originally had in mind, he proposed a number of modifications that would put his personal stamp on the building that Washington and Hoban created. To make sure his plans were followed, he dismissed Hoban, who had supervised the project for nearly nine years. In his place, he installed his own architect, Benjamin Latrobe.

MAIN FLOOR PLAN

The basic floor plan of the "state floor" that Hoban designed has survived, with few changes, for two centuries. Just as in Adams's time, there are five rooms on the main floor in the central portion that host all public functions at the White House.

The largest of these is the East Room, a spacious hall with twenty-two-foot ceilings, which was originally designed by Hoban as the "Public Audience Room." Although it has been used for humble purposes, such as the laundry room for Abigail Adams and the rollerskating hall for Theodore Roosevelt's young boys, the East Room has also been the site of momentous and somber occasions. The bodies of the seven presidents who died in office, including assassinated presidents Abraham Lincoln and John Kennedy, lay in state in this room while the mourning public filed by to pay their respects. The East Room also hosts major receptions, press conferences, and after-dinner entertainment.

The State Dining Room is the only room on the main floor to undergo significant alteration. Originally thirty feet by thirty-five feet, the room quickly proved far too cramped to host the kind of public dinners required of the chief of state. It has since been expanded to serve 140 guests.

The other three main rooms of the state floor are smaller reception rooms known by their colors—the Green Room, the Red Room, and the Blue Room. Thomas Jefferson unwittingly started this color tradition. Not wanting to damage the beautiful new floor in the small alcove next to the East Room, he had it covered

In an early inspection, Latrobe was shocked to find that the house was beginning to fall apart even before it was completed. The decision to install a slate roof had been disastrous. Too heavy for the framework to support, already the crushing weight of the slate was causing the upper rear and front walls to spread apart. Structurally unsound, the roof failed to keep out the rain. So much water had leaked into the ceiling of the East Room that it was on the verge of collapsing. Latrobe had to tear out the old roof and replace it with one of painted sheet iron.

The most drastic of Jefferson's designs was his plan to extend both wings of the house so far that they would connect with a large piece of green canvas. Those familiar with the White House commonly referred to it as the Green Room.

Dolley Madison, who was serving as Jefferson's White House hostess, then established the theme of a series of distinctively colored rooms when she bought bright red curtains for the small sitting room near the State Dining Room.

Not everyone was pleased with her taste in decorating this room. *The White House: An Historic Guide* quotes Latrobe as complaining, "The curtains! Oh, the terrible velvet curtains! Their effect will ruin me so brilliant will they be!" Nonetheless, the tradition of

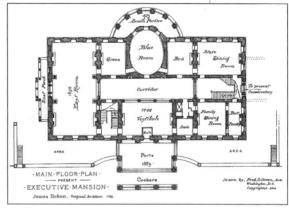

The main floor plan of the White House, including the large East Room at left.

the colored rooms has carried on to the present time.

Eventually, blue was chosen as the theme for the largest of the three reception rooms, the oval-shaped room that extends into the bay windows of the south porch. This area serves as the main reception room for guests of the president. The Red and Green Rooms which flank the Blue Room are used for special occasions.

with the new executive buildings several hundred feet away. Contradicting his early preference for simplicity, the president envisioned embellishing the wings with majestic arches. Work on this project began in 1805.

As with his original entry in the President's House contest, Jefferson let creativity override practicality. In order to fulfill the president's wishes, workers had to stay on the project until late in the fall of 1806, past the time when they normally would have quit for the winter. The weather was so cold when the masons constructed the arches that the mortar would not set. When the supports were pulled away, the arches cracked and fell apart. Jefferson and Latrobe had to

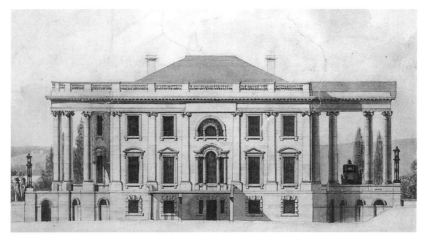

Latrobe's 1807 drawing includes the north portico (right) and south portico (left). The porticoes were not actually completed until 1828.

settle for shorter and less ambitious wings that included pavilions and low terraces on both ends; construction was completed in 1807.

Jefferson's other major change involved the main stairs from the main floor to the second floor. Hoban had designed a grand central stairway that dominated the great hall. At Jefferson's request, Latrobe left the center of the room open and installed a pair of stairs that climbed along the walls. Jefferson also directed Latrobe to change Hoban's few spacious bedrooms into a series of smaller bedrooms, each of which had its own dressing room.

The design of the President's House was completed during Jefferson's second term, at which time the mansion was reasonably well furnished. From that point, Jefferson's only significant contributions to the home were his inventions of convenience, such as various dumbwaiters to hoist food from the kitchen to the dining room so that he and his guests would not have their conversation interrupted by servants. He cared little for entertaining or decorating. In the words of one White House visitor, Jefferson "inhabits but a corner of the mansion himself, and abandons the rest to a state of uncleanly desolation."[20] Jefferson left the finishing touches to his successor, James Madison. Madison, who had no more interest in such things than Jefferson, left it to his wife, Dolley, to work with Latrobe on arranging and decorating the mansion in style.

FIRE AND REBUILDING

With the charming Dolley Madison in control, the President's House finally began to emerge as George Washington had envisioned it—a stately centerpiece and majestic symbol of a confident nation. Along with the bold Capitol building, the President's House served notice that the United States was an independent nation that would endure among the world powers for centuries. Washington would have been heartsick to know that these two buildings, in which he had invested so much time, effort, and hope, would be burnt and nearly destroyed within fifteen years of his death.

TROUBLE BREWING

Relations between the United States and Great Britain had been cool since the American Revolution. Ill will intensified as the war between Great Britain and the French army of Napoléon raged into the nineteenth century. Both combatants placed a blockade on any shipping between neutral countries and their enemy. This greatly hurt merchants in the United States, who had been enjoying a flourishing trade with both countries.

The British attack the American ship Chesapeake.

Great Britain went a step further and declared its right to board American vessels and impress, or forcibly take, sailors who had deserted the British navy and signed on with U.S. vessels. In June 1807, a British warship fired on the USS *Chesapeake,* forcing it to submit to boarding. The British took away four men whom they declared deserters and hanged one of them.

The United States was outraged by what it considered a blatant violation of its sovereignty (the right to govern its own affairs). Jefferson's administration tried a number of diplomatic tactics to strike back, including an embargo that banned all commerce between the United States and Great Britain. Such efforts, however, were ineffective. The embargo hurt the U.S. economy at least as much as it hurt the British.

Great Britain's refusal to change its impressment policy, along with suspicion and evidence that it was sending arms to Indians through Canada and encouraging them to fight U.S. settlers, finally exhausted the patience of the Madison administration. On June 1, 1812, President Madison asked Congress to declare war on Great Britain. Had he waited just a little longer, the problem would have been solved peacefully. Two days before Madison's request, the British government had agreed to modify its high-handed naval policy, but the news did not reach the United States until after hostilities had begun.

BRITISH INVASION

The Americans' main objective in the war was to conquer British-controlled Canada. Unfortunately, Jefferson had virtually ignored the military during his administration. Wary of a strong central government, he had failed to provide for a trained federal army of any size. The poorly equipped, disorganized U.S. forces that repeatedly attempted to invade Canada failed miserably.

One of their few successes came in April 1813, when they captured York (present-day Toronto), the capital of lower Canada. The Americans were quickly driven out of York. But during their brief control of the city, their soldiers blew up and set fire to military stores in the city. Several government buildings burned in the process.

The British were outraged by the destruction of the buildings. Planning to invade the American East Coast to draw attention away from Canada, they focused on Washington, D.C. Determined to give the impudent Americans a taste of their own medicine, they sent an expedition led by Rear Admiral Sir George Cockburn of the navy and Major General Robert Ross of the army to Chesapeake Bay.

Jefferson had left the U.S. Navy in no better shape than the army. The commander of the tiny U.S. fleet guarding Chesapeake Bay realized he had no chance of defeating the approaching British. Rather than allow the British to capture his fleet, he removed the cannon and blew up the ships.

Cockburn and Ross sailed up the Patuxent River, northeast of Washington, D.C., and dispatched four thousand troops to make the short overland march to their objective. The United States desperately tried to gather an army to throw into the field to stop the British march.

FLIGHT FROM THE PRESIDENT'S HOUSE

President Madison rushed out to inspect the battle preparations, leaving Dolley to prepare for the grim possibility that the President's House would have to be evacuated. She spent much of the day supervising the packing of important belongings. At the urging of Secretary of State James Monroe, workers at the Capitol and other federal buildings scrambled to save important government documents.

On August 24, 1814, the two armies collided in one-hundred-degree heat at Bladensburg, Maryland, just five miles from the capital. The battle did not last long. Despite outnumbering the British nearly two to one, the poorly organized U.S. Army fled the field without putting up much of a fight.

Reports of Dolley Madison's actions during the frantic moments following the start of the battle vary. According to her own account, she shuddered as she heard the sounds of cannon and tried to view the action from the President's House windows with a spyglass. Twice messengers raced to the President's House from the battlefield, urging her to leave at once. She insisted to both that she would wait for the president to arrive before fleeing. Frantically, she collected the president's papers and as many cabinet documents as she could. There was no time to save any personal belongings other than some velvet curtains, a few books, and a massive portrait of George Washington. With the British advancing perilously

James Madison asked Congress to declare war on Great Britain in 1812.

GILBERT STUART'S PAINTING

The one President's House furnishing that Dolley Madison was determined to save was a portrait of George Washington by the famous painter Gilbert Stuart. The painting was so massive and unwieldy that unscrewing it from its wall mounting proved to be a time-consuming effort at a moment when time was of the essence.

Stuart's famous painting of Washington.

The White House: An Historic Guide quotes Mrs. Madison describing her solution to the problem in a letter she composed as she was making her final preparations to leave the President's House: "I have ordered the frame to be broken, and the canvas taken out: it is done, and the precious portrait placed in the hands of two gentlemen from New York, for safe keeping. And now, dear sister, I must leave this house, or the retreating army will make me a prisoner in it."

The New York gentlemen were Robert de Peyster and Jacob Barker, who happened to be visiting the President's House. Mrs. Madison asked them to destroy the portrait rather than let the British capture it. De Peyster and Barker hauled the enormous canvas to a farmhouse west of Georgetown, where it stayed hidden for a few weeks until the British threat was defeated. The portrait was eventually returned to the President's House, where it remains today—the only surviving object from the original President's House.

close to the city, and her husband still nowhere to be seen, she finally departed.

Other accounts say that Dolley was making arrangements for dinner when she heard the sound of cannon coming from much closer than expected. Fearing the British were charging into the outskirts of the city, she cut short the evacuation of personal belongings and fled. The president returned to the house in the early evening to find almost everyone gone. Realizing that nothing could halt the British advance, he too fled to safety.

As soon as the house was abandoned, a mob that had assembled near the scene broke in and helped themselves to the furnishings.

THE PRESIDENT'S HOUSE BURNS

The mob had little time for looting because the British army followed closely on Madison's heels. British troops reached the Capitol early in the evening, while Madison was taking leave of the President's House. After setting fire to the Capitol, they marched to the President's House, arriving around 10:30 P.M.

The soldiers stripped the house of any remaining valuables. According to one account, a soldier "exchanged his dirty underclothes for fresh garments belonging to the President of the United States."[21] The officers then dined at the table that had been set for the president's return from Bladensburg.

Major General Ross then ordered glowing embers to be brought from a nearby tavern. The soldiers lit torches from

British soldiers march through Washington, D.C., on August 24, 1814, leaving a destroyed capital in their wake.

these, and between 11 P.M. and midnight began setting fire to anything in the house that would burn. By 12:30 A.M. fire was raging throughout the house.

It would have burned to the ground were it not for the timely intervention of a storm so severe that many historians believe it was a full-scale hurricane. There were reports of roofs being blown off buildings and heavy cannon being tossed about like empty boxes. The British, made nervous by the approach of another American force coming up from Virginia, could not wait to make certain the fire did its work. After they set off in the middle of the night in search of shelter, the torrential rains doused the fire.

Although the stone of the upper story was cracked, and the stone on the west wall badly damaged, the white walls of the exterior remained standing, like a bleached skeleton surrounding a mansion that was entirely gutted. The roof was burned away. Everything inside the building was totally destroyed.

STARTING OVER

The British army expected that the ease with which they had marched into and burned the U.S. capital would collapse American resistance. Instead, the people, humiliated by the British actions, rose up with a fury. Ross's army was hounded throughout the countryside by U.S. troops. By the time the soldiers made it back to their ships and sailed away, Ross had lost nearly a quarter of his men to battle casualties, sickness, and desertion.

For President Madison, the loss of the President's House was the most devastating setback of his career. One observer described the president as "miserably shattered and woebegone. In short, he looks heartbroken."[22]

The Madisons moved into temporary quarters at a small nearby residence called the Octagon House. Built in 1800, it had served as the home of the French ambassador. Eventually, they moved to what was commonly called the Seven Buildings, on Pennsylvania Avenue, not far from the President's House, where Madison finished out his term.

Meanwhile, a lively debate took place over what to do about the charred President's House. Many people questioned the location of Washington, D.C. The British attack had ex-

DISASTER THAT HELPED BRING A NATION TOGETHER

 Prior to the British attack on Washington, D.C., the United States had been deeply split in its decision to wage war. The southern and western states took the greatest exception to Great Britain's high-handed behavior on the seas. The passions of western settlers were further inflamed by British involvement in Indian disputes along the northwestern frontier.

The New England states, however, feared that war with Great Britain was a mistake that would ruin their shipping business and cost the nation its newly won independence. The Federalist Party, which was strong in that part of the country, was so firm in its opposition to the war that it referred to the fighting as "Mr. Madison's War." Many New England towns refused to provide soldiers, sailors, or ships for the U.S. war effort.

The British army hoped that the ease with which it had captured and destroyed the U.S. capital would bring the Americans crawling on their knees to a treaty conference. Instead, the burning of the federal buildings shocked and disgusted even many British citizens who prided themselves in the civilized behavior of their troops. Even the most ardent war opponents in the United States were stung by the insult to the nation's dignity, particularly the vindictive burning of the president's personal residence. Almost overnight, opposition to the war melted away. The Federalist Party, which had taken a firm stand against the war, lost all credibility and disappeared from the U.S. political scene.

For the first time in the nation's brief history, all regions of the country joined together in their support of the federal government.

posed the vulnerability of a site so close to the sea. What would prevent the British, the world's dominant naval power, from repeating their insult whenever they felt like teaching the United States a lesson? Congress debated whether the capital should be moved to a location farther inland where it would be safe

The President's House after the fire of 1814. Although the exterior was left standing, the fire claimed the roof and everything inside the building.

from seafaring raids. Cincinnati, along the Ohio River, emerged as the favored new location.

Others wanted to rebuild the capital on its present site. They feared a repeat of the frustrating squabbles that tore the country the last time they debated where to put the federal buildings. Furthermore, they felt that moving the capital would be a surrender to the bullying British. The U.S. Army's decisive victory over British troops in New Orleans in the final battle of the war helped settle the question. With its confidence restored, the United States defiantly chose to rebuild its capital just as it was before the British invasion.

Madison was one of the foremost advocates of this decision. As badly damaged as the President's House was, the president wanted it restored to the way it was rather than starting from scratch. He often referred to the rebuilding as simply a "repair."

HOBAN RETURNS

Benjamin Latrobe assumed that he would be given the responsibility of restoring the President's House. But he lasted only a brief time on the job before his political enemies succeeded in having him removed. In March 1815, federal officials turned to the man who knew more about the President's House construction than anyone else, James Hoban, the original builder. Supervising a work crew made up largely of Scots and Italians, Hoban cleared out the debris and rebuilt the interior walls almost exactly as they

DOLLEY MADISON

Dolley Madison served as hostess of the President's House longer than any other woman in history. She began her duties well before her husband, James, won election as president. Thomas Jefferson, a widower who disliked large, formal gatherings, needed someone to supervise receptions and other formal social events. Seventeen years younger than her serious, bookish husband, Dolley had earned a widespread reputation as an elegant hostess. Her social skills and her position as wife of Jefferson's trusted secretary of state made her the obvious choice for taking over the official hostessing during his two terms of office. Dolley continued to direct activities at the President's House during the six years of her husband's term prior to the burning by the British.

A portrait of Dolley Madison by Gilbert Stuart.

Mrs. Madison was not considered particularly beautiful. Her charm lay in her irresistible smile, upbeat spirits, and gift for putting both friends and strangers at ease in any setting. Dressed in the elaborate turbans that were her trademark, she flitted from guest to guest making sure everyone felt welcome.

Dolley Madison was so much a part of the Washington social scene that she returned to the city following James's death in 1836. She remained an admired fixture of government social functions until her death at the age of eighty-one.

had been originally. The improvements he made were in the quality of work, not design. For example, the wooden beams he installed to support the second floor were so strong that they would last until 1949.

Hoban completed the rebuilding in 1817. In January of the following year, President James Monroe was finally able to move from his residence at the Octagon House to the President's House.

THE PORTICOES

The one major design change that Hoban included in the rebuilding of the President's House was the addition of two elegant porticoes, or porches. He drew plans for one on the south entrance and one on the north.

The north portico of the White House was added in 1828.

Historians have had difficulty determining who was responsible for the original design of the porticoes. Some claim that Jefferson came up with the idea in the early discussions of the proposed house. Others believe that Latrobe developed the concept, which he included in his 1807 floor plans for finishing the building. Still others insist that Latrobe was merely fleshing out an idea that Hoban had originally worked out during his consultations with Washington. Regardless of the origin of the idea, Jefferson approved the additions of the porticoes during his administration but found other matters took priority over their inclusion. Those plans were not revived until 1816 during the rebuilding of the burned President's House. Seale concludes the matter by saying, "Whatever the concept for this addition, the final design and execution were Hoban's."[23]

As in Jefferson's time, the addition of the porticoes was put off during reconstruction following the fire. Perpetually short of funds, federal officials were reluctant to fund the construction of what was essentially a cosmetic feature with no practical value. In the early 1820s, they reconsidered the matter and agreed to go ahead.

The south portico came first, in 1824, during the final years of Monroe's administration. It is actually both a porch and an elaborate staircase. Construction of the north portico was delayed for several years, primarily because of political bickering. John Quincy Adams was elected president in 1824 despite winning fewer popular votes than Andrew Jackson. Bitter about what they considered a stolen election, Jackson's supporters in Congress refused to cooperate with Adams. Among their more petty actions was the denial of funds for the maintenance of the President's House. Adams could not even get money to replace broken windowpanes, much less funds for any new additions. Immediately after Jackson defeated Adams in the 1828 election, Congress freed up the money and construction of the north portico proceeded.

The two creative embellishments to the main entrances have survived intact to this day, the only alteration being the addition by Harry Truman of a porch midway up the north portico. They are the features that give the building its distinctive look today.

RENOVATIONS: THE FIRST CENTURY

Although its main part has remained largely intact since it was rebuilt for Monroe, the White House has always been a work in progress. Because the building is a private residence as well as a government building, presidents and their wives have traditionally been given freedom to make alterations in it to suit their needs, tastes, and lifestyles. Following Monroe's decision to fill the new White House with expensive French furniture, all presidential families have put their personal stamp on the White House, by redecorating, refurnishing, or updating the facilities.

A few have managed to institute major changes and renovations. Many more have tried but were unable to accomplish their goals. The problem has been that any extensive remodeling of such an enormous house costs a great deal of money, far more than most presidents are able or willing to pay out of pocket. All presidents have been dependent upon Congress to provide money for the changes they desired. Some have benefited from a generous allowance from Congress, while others have been given no choice but to make do with limited resources.

RUNDOWN PALACE

Were it not for the lavish allowance that he received from his supporters in Congress, Andrew Jackson would have either left the President's House in a shambles or gone bankrupt trying to maintain it. Widely hailed as a champion of the common people, Jackson wanted to rid the federal government of any upper-class trappings. In keeping with this philosophy, he declared that federal buildings, including the President's House, were public property. Therefore, any citizen was welcome to visit without an invitation.

Many working-class people took Jackson at his word. Jackson's presidential home was often overrun by visitors, many of them ill-mannered. Eight years of almost constant abuse by hundreds of curious people left most of the public areas worn, dirty, and tattered.

Strongly supported in Congress, Jackson had no difficulty getting money for the expenditures he requested for the President's House. It was his successors who would pay for the damage inflicted by his exuberant and careless visitors. Martin Van Buren, Jackson's vice president and successor in office, discovered that popularity and not need dictated what a president could spend on upkeep of the President's House. Van Buren had none of Jackson's personal magnetism. When he submitted a modest request for funds to replace and repair some of the damaged items, Congress ridiculed him for trying to waste taxpayers' money. Pennsylvania congressman Charles Ogle scoffed that Van Buren was already living in a "palace as splendid as that of the Caesars"[24] and yet was not satisfied.

Andrew Jackson declared the President's House public property.

Congress maintained its tight-fisted policy throughout the first half of the nineteenth century. According to Ryan and Guiness, "The interior of the President's House reached its nadir [lowest point] during the administration of John Tyler."[25] A political lightweight who became president only because of the death of William Henry Harrison, Tyler had no more support in Congress than John Quincy Adams had received. Although the President's House was falling into a state of severe dilapidation, Congress refused to give him a cent for its maintenance.

MINOR ADDITIONS

Until the presidency of Ulysses Grant in the 1870s, the only additions made to the White House were extremely minor. For example, Abigail Fillmore, a former schoolteacher, was determined that the nation's chief executive should have a library, and she raised private funds to establish one. James Buchanan built a small greenhouse on the roof of the west wing.

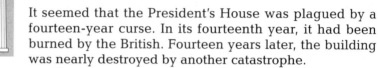

JACKSON'S INAUGURATION PARTY

It seemed that the President's House was plagued by a fourteen-year curse. In its fourteenth year, it had been burned by the British. Fourteen years later, the building was nearly destroyed by another catastrophe.

The occasion was President Jackson's inauguration party. The president's appeal to the common citizen attracted many hard-living, hard-partying folks who were ecstatic over Jackson's election. Accepting Jackson's open invitation to the inauguration celebration, they poured into the President's House. Whooping and shouting with delight, many of them tromped through the house in their muddy boots. Not only did they ruin the expensive rugs, but they climbed onto the exquisitely upholstered chairs and couches in their attempts to get a view of the president, who was mobbed by the crowd.

Security was lax and the heavy-drinking partiers quickly surged out of control. Fights broke out and furniture was smashed. Greedy visitors cut pieces of drapery and upholstery to take home as souvenirs. A crowd poured into the East Room, where they started what amounted to a food fight, destroying refreshments and smashing dishes and glasses. At one point the crowd grew so violent that Jackson's aides feared for his safety. They whisked him through the crowd and helped him escape through a back door.

Although the house was a shambles by the time the revelers cleared out early in the morning, all things considered, the federal officials were thankful it was still standing.

Crowds swarm the President's House for Andrew Jackson's 1828 inauguration party.

Abraham Lincoln resisted his wife's efforts to spruce up the decaying house. With so many of the nation's families making terrible sacrifices to preserve the Union in the Civil War, he did not feel it proper to spend taxpayer money on his own comfort. Nonetheless, Mary Lincoln was able to get $20,000 from Congress to refurbish the mansion. A lavish spender, she went well over budget on her purchases, a fact that she tried to hide from the president. When he found out, Lincoln felt obligated to pay the difference himself until he discovered that her overspending was far more than he could afford. Sheepishly, he had to ask Congress for additional funds.

Lincoln's compassion added considerably to the hard use suffered by the White House. He could not resist opening up the East Room as a barracks for Union soldiers who had no decent place to sleep during their weeks of training in Washington. The only money Lincoln spent himself on the building was for the construction of a private passageway so that he could get from his reception room to his office without having to wade through the crowds that regularly gathered at the White House.

GRANT SAVES THE WHITE HOUSE

By the time Andrew Johnson took over for the assassinated Lincoln in 1865, the White House was an embarrassment to both its occupants and visitors. In July 1866, a Senate committee on public buildings and grounds looked into the possibility of replacing it altogether. Several possible sites in and around the city of Washington were considered, and the committee ordered a study of the costs of buying the land. The site that won the most support was on the summit of a hill located on a portion of the Moncure Robinson estate, a few miles northeast of the Capitol.

Abraham Lincoln used the East Room to house Union soldiers.

Officials went as far as ordering plans for a new house on that spot, under the supervision of military engineer General Michler. Before anything more could be done, however, a bitter feud between Johnson and the Republicans who controlled Congress led to the impeachment of the president. Although the Senate acquitted Johnson of the charges by a single vote, the simmering hostility between the president and Congress ended any chance of the project going forward.

The proposed move was revived when war hero Ulysses Grant won the presidency in 1868. His superintendent of buildings and grounds, Orville Babcock, who was responsible for upkeep of the building, stated, "It hardly seems possible to state anything in favor of the house as a residence."[26] However, tradition was far more important than modern convenience to the no-frills, plain-living Grants. Julia Grant loved the White House, and her husband flatly refused to consider building a new presidential house.

The White House was in such poor condition, however, that something had to be done to save it. Grant agreed to an extensive refurbishing, which began in 1873. Cracked ceilings were fixed and rotten timbers replaced. The East Room was completely redecorated. To gain more hall space, the president had Jefferson's double stair torn out and replaced with a single one, according to Hoban's original design.

Ulysses S. Grant opposed building a new presidential house.

ARTHUR'S RENOVATION

Rutherford Hayes, Grant's successor, was a man of simple tastes and lifestyle. He and his wife pronounced the White House perfectly satisfactory to their needs. The man who followed him, James Garfield, was assassinated shortly after taking office. That brought his vice president, Chester Alan Arthur, into the picture.

A wealthy widower who was used to living in style, Arthur found the state of the building so appalling that he appealed to Congress to build a new house for him. When Congress balked, he substituted a proposal for building a new residential wing onto the White House. This plan came close to achieving success, winning approval in the Senate. The House of Representatives, however, blocked the plan.

Unable to relocate or redesign the White House, Arthur had to settle for refurbishing the existing structure. Showing what many considered a callous disdain for history, he had twenty-four wagonloads of White House furnishings hauled away and sold at public auctions. (Arthur's estimate of the value of the furnishings was vindicated by the rock-bottom prices offered by bidders.) He commissioned the famed New York artist and decorator Louis Tiffany to redecorate the entire White House from top to bottom. Tiffany filled the building with artwork, added intricate stenciling and glazing to the walls, and filled the rooms with new and reupholstered furniture. The work was finished in December of 1881.

CARRIE HARRISON'S AMBITIOUS PLAN

While the expensive redecorating pleased Arthur, it failed to impress his successors. Grover Cleveland almost immediately submitted his own plans for remodeling. Having spent a great deal to satisfy Arthur, Congress was in no mood to comply. Cleveland responded by being the only U.S. president in history to voluntarily use his own Washington home as his main residence during the bulk of his presidency.

After one term of office, Cleveland was defeated by Benjamin Harrison. Benjamin and Carrie Harrison brought with them a large extended family that included their two married children, their small grandchildren, and Carrie's sister, niece, and ninety-year-old father. All of them had to squeeze into the five bedrooms available to them on the second floor.

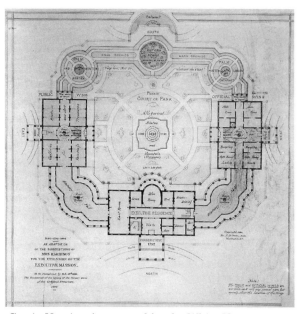

Carrie Harrison's proposal for the White House expansion, drawn by architect Fred D. Owen.

The living arrangement so frustrated the First Lady that she undertook a campaign to completely redesign the White House. Her plans were the most drastic changes ever seriously proposed for the building. She envisioned extending the wings into a giant quadrangle that would enclose a vast

PRIVACY

One of the things that most bothered Carrie Harrison about the White House was the lack of privacy. During the early years of the building this had not been a problem. Both John Adams and Thomas Jefferson acknowledged that the home had far more room than they could hope to use. But over the years, the White House staff had steadily grown in size until the families began to feel squeezed into an increasingly small corner of the building. This was especially true for presidents with large extended families, such as the Harrisons, or those with children, such as the Theodore Roosevelt family.

First Lady Carrie Harrison.

As the living quarters became more cramped, the problems of trying to maintain privacy in a public building became more serious. Carrie Harrison was especially irked that the White House provided only one private bathroom for the entire family. The Theodore Roosevelts had a great deal of trouble keeping their boisterous boys from charging into solemn ceremonies or upsetting formal preparations.

Even with the many enlargements and improvements of the White House over the years, the issue of privacy continued to be a sore spot. One problem that was not addressed for more than a century and a half was the family dining situation. Since the early days of the White House, the families had to go down to a small dining room on the first floor to eat their meals. This was necessary because the food was prepared in the basement kitchen, and it was a long enough haul from there to the first floor. In the early 1960s, however, Jacqueline Kennedy solved the problem by converting a bedroom into a small kitchen that could serve the family in their private second floor dining area.

Mrs. Kennedy's successor, Lady Bird Johnson, found that the family could not even find seclusion in their private rooms. After going for a swim in the White House pool, Mrs. Johnson put on a bathrobe and retreated to the bedroom. Not expecting to see anyone, she had not bothered to dry her hair. The First Lady shrieked upon finding a group of Lyndon Johnson's advisors gathered around the president, discussing policy.

courtyard. The original, central portion of the house would primarily be taken over by the family. A new wing extending to the south from the west side would house the official government functions and connect with the main portion of the house by an ornately embellished corridor.

Parallel to this, on the east side, she proposed a "National Wing," which would be primarily a gallery displaying some of the nation's finest artwork. Both wings would be connected on the south by a conservatory.

A bill authorizing the changes proposed by Carrie Harrison was introduced in the House of Representatives. Historians believe it would have had a good chance of passing had not a very minor oversight escalated into a feud between the president and Speaker of the House Thomas Reed. Harrison neglected to make a political appointment in Reed's home district in Maine prior to the scheduled hearing on the bill. Reed, who controlled the House agenda so tightly that he was nicknamed "Czar" Reed, got even by blocking Carrie's bill.

By the time Reed was in a mood to accommodate the White House, the opportunity had passed. Carrie Harrison died during her husband's term, and with the champion of the quadrangle plan gone, the campaign fizzled.

PUT OFF NO LONGER

Returning to office in 1893, Grover Cleveland again skirted the problem of an inadequate White House by spending most of his time at his other residence. William McKinley then tried to pick up where Carrie Harrison had left off, with a major redesign. The proposal he endorsed was nearly as drastic a change as Harrison's. Although the south wing that formed Harrison's quadrangle was eliminated, his version included the construction of a larger wing at each end of the existing building. The plan called for the corridors to be covered with domes and for huge half-moon windows at the end of each wing.

Again, fate intervened. McKinley was assassinated before his proposals got anywhere. In his place came the youngest man ever to assume the presidency, Theodore Roosevelt. For the first time in history, a man with a large family of very active youngsters took up residence in the White House. The clash between the dignified, formal function of the building

Theodore Roosevelt and his four sons, (clockwise from top) Theodore Jr., Archibald, Quentin, and Kermit.

and its informal function as a private home became unmanageable in its existing condition.

Something had to be done immediately. Congress realized it had no choice but to accept major changes in the White House. Roosevelt now held the power of choice that all presidents since the time of Arthur had wanted. He could initiate the sort of major changes in the building that Harrison and McKinley had tried; move altogether as the Army Corps of Engineers had been advising for decades; or try to work changes in the existing structure.

Renovations: The Second Century

Theodore Roosevelt was both a man with a keen sense of pride in the nation's history and a decisive leader. In response to a reporter's question about yet another movement among federal officials to build a new president's house, Roosevelt snapped, "You tell the newspapermen that Mrs. Roosevelt and I are firmly of the opinion that the president shall live nowhere else than in the historic White House!"[27] While he realized the President's House was badly outdated and no longer adequate, he was determined to preserve it in something close to its original form as a tribute to those who had gone before him. He insisted that whatever changes and additions the architects made would complement the existing structure.

Charles McKim, founding partner of the most successful American architectural firm at the time, accepted responsibility for the project in 1902. McKim had earned a reputation for excellence with such building designs as the Boston Public Library and the Pennsylvania Railroad Station in New York City. But never in his life was he asked to do so much in so little time. Unwilling to inconvenience himself or his family for an extended period, the impatient Roosevelt allowed McKim only five months to accomplish the work. Even under such a time restriction, the president seemingly expected McKim to work around his normal routine. For while the family moved to temporary quarters on Lafayette Square during the remodeling, the president at first continued working at his White House office. Eventually, though, the plaster dust became unbearable, and Roosevelt grudgingly abandoned his post.

Three Main Projects

Wherever possible, McKim strove not just to restore what presently existed, but to return it to its original state. That meant clearing out the clutter of the conservatory, greenhouses, stalls,

PLAYGROUND OF THE WHITE HOUSE GANG

Most families moving into the White House find it worn from the hard use of the previous tenants. No occupants were harder on the building than the family of Theodore Roosevelt. The main culprits were the three younger boys, Kermit (twelve years old on entering the White House), Archie (seven), and Quentin (four). Along with three of their friends, they were known as the White House Gang, and they treated the building as their personal playground. Among their favorite tricks was to follow the White House lamplighter as he made his rounds through the property. The boys enjoyed seeing how many freshly lit candles they could blow out before they were caught.

The boys' father did nothing to discourage them; in fact, by most accounts, he was as guilty of roughhousing as any of them. Pillow fights between the president and his children were a regular event. In *A Bully Father* by Joan Paterson Kerr, one of the White House Gang told the story of how the president took a break from a meeting in order to scuffle with them in the attic. Roosevelt showed up in his shirtsleeves and proceeded to chase the boys around the attic, growling fiercely. During the chase, one of the boys flipped off the light switch. In the darkness that followed, they heard a loud thump as the president crashed into a pillar.

"By George! By George! Lights! Lights!" howled Roosevelt. "This is worse than anything I've ever heard of in darkest Africa."

sheds, and other appendages that presidents had erected over the years. Rather than perform a room-by-room renovation as had been done during Arthur's administration, McKim considered the building as a whole. How could he make the place more efficient and usable?

McKim's work involved three main projects. The first was to go through the entire building to make sure it was structurally sound. This led him to replace all of the floors in the main building.

Second, in order to give the president's family more living space, McKim moved the presidential offices out of the second floor of the main building. As Washington and Jefferson had envisioned, and many presidents had tried to accomplish, he added space by extending both wings. He constructed a new

The boys quickly switched the light back on. They were horrified to see the president had narrowly missed a post with a nail sticking out of it at eye level.

When they were not luring their father into their mischief, the White House Gang often enlisted employees as accomplices. On an occasion when Archie was sick with the measles, Quentin knew just what to do to cheer him up. With the aid of a White House coachman, he pushed his pony, Algonquin, into the elevator, and walked him into the room where his brother lay ill.

Archie (right) and Quentin Roosevelt blow bubbles.

Such disregard for the house was typical of the Roosevelt boys. Once, near the end of Theodore's presidency, Quentin and his friend Charlie Taft (son of Roosevelt's handpicked successor) were banging around even more recklessly than usual. Mrs. Roosevelt scolded them. According to Joan Paterson Kerr in *A Bully Father,* "Quentin responded that it was all right, as Charlie Taft would soon be in this house anyway, so what difference did it make if he tore it to pieces."

executive wing on the west side of the building to house the president's office, the Cabinet room, press room, and secretarial offices. At the same time, he made room in the east wing for cloakrooms and restrooms.

With the offices moved out, and visitors' facilities installed elsewhere, the president's family would finally have the second floor entirely to themselves. The former offices were converted into enough bedrooms to accommodate even a large family such as the Roosevelts. Four new bathrooms were installed on the residential floor in addition to the three that already existed.

The third major project addressed the need for more efficient management of crowds at government functions. The most glaring need was enlarging the State Dining Room. McKim had forty-one feet of brick wall removed so that the room could be

The State Dining Room after architect Charles McKim's 1902 renovations. The dining room was expanded twenty feet.

expanded twenty feet into the former hallway. He compensated for the lost space in the hall by taking out one of the stairways. The grand stairway was relocated to where the smaller office stair had been.

THE WHITE HOUSE IS SAVED

Despite the ambitious workload placed on him, McKim satisfied his demanding boss by finishing the bulk of the work by December 1902, ahead of schedule and under budget. It was a remarkable accomplishment. In the opinion of William Seale, "Few adaptations of historic American buildings have been more successful than this."[28]

Roosevelt's plan, and the skill with which McKim carried out the work, preserved the President's House as one of the centerpieces of the U.S. government. Thanks to Roosevelt's sense of history, the main portion of the Executive Mansion looks much the same today as it has throughout its existence. Since Roosevelt took his stand, no succeeding president has made a serious effort either to remove or dramatically alter the structure's appearance. Roosevelt further solidified the building's status as a national treasure by officially bestowing on it the title that average Americans had been using for nearly one hundred years: the White House.

THE OVAL OFFICE

On succeeding Roosevelt in 1908, William Howard Taft found one loose end that McKim had failed to tie up in his remodeling of the White House. The location of the president's office had never been settled. Roosevelt had retained an office in the main building as a matter of convenience but had also used a temporary office in the west wing, especially during construction in the main building. Neither office was particularly impressive.

Taft decided to construct a new, permanent presidential office in the executive west wing. He wanted the office to be distinctive and so on April 29, 1909, he announced a contest for its design. The winner was architect Nathan C. Wyeth, who gave the room the kind of special identity Taft was seeking by designing it in the shape of an oval. Work on the Oval Office began in October 1909, in the center of the west wing, taking over the spot where the presidential secretary's office had been.

Ironically, although he often used the office during his working hours, Taft found himself attached to the old office. He could not bring himself to break tradition and so he always returned to the old office to sign treaties or bills.

The Oval Office was constructed in 1909.

Woodrow Wilson carried on that tradition for a while, and so no official ceremonies were held in the Oval Office until following World War I.

In 1934, Franklin Roosevelt had the president's office moved to the southeast corner of the executive wing, closer to the main building. From there, presidents could more easily gain access to the room from their private residence. In fact, an underground passage has since been constructed that allows the president to move directly between the office and the residence without having to go through any other rooms or halls.

COOLIDGE AND THE THIRD FLOOR

While his remodeling design was a work of genius, McKim made a costly error. In enlarging the State Dining Room, he had misjudged the amount of support needed to hold up the upper floors and roof. In 1923 the Army Corps of Engineers informed President Calvin Coolidge that repairs would have to be performed. The notoriously frugal Coolidge resisted having the work done, but eventually the falling plaster convinced him that the building was not safe.

The Coolidges moved to a house on DuPont Circle in March 1927, and construction workers rebuilt what used to be the attic into a third story. Although this raised the roofline somewhat, architects took care to prevent changing the building's appearance. They installed a skeleton of steel and concrete resting on the old masonry shell of building and walls.

The enlargement of the third floor nearly doubled the amount of private living space in the house. Most of this was used to provide guest rooms and servants' quarters.

PIANO LEG THROUGH THE FLOOR

Following the Japanese surprise attack on Pearl Harbor in 1941, U.S. government officials worried about the possibility of a similar attack on the White House. As a safety precaution, they ordered a complete inspection of the building to gauge its vulnerability to bombing and fire. The inspectors were shocked and dismayed at the deteriorating condition of the building. Yet little was done until President Harry Truman got a harsh wakeup call in the summer of 1948. One of the legs of a grand piano belonging to his daughter Margaret suddenly broke through two floorboards and knocked plaster off the ceiling of the family dining room below.

The problem could be ignored no longer. Another inspection uncovered a host of problems. In the wry words of one engineer, "It is a wonderful thing to contemplate the abuse that materials of construction sometimes will undergo before failure."[29]

It seemed that in their efforts to make the White House both safe and livable, the experts had continually solved one problem by creating others. The walls, beams, and joists had been cut into so often over many decades to add such modern conveniences as electrical wiring, plumbing pipes, and gas connections that they resembled honeycombs. In the 1927 enlargement of the third floor, engineers had failed to take into account the vastly weakened condition of the interior supports and had woefully miscalculated the amount of weight they could hold. Some of the floors were starting to sag badly. Several rooms now sported deep cracks in the plaster from the floor to the ceiling. Experts warned that the entire building was crumbling.

By November of that year, Truman and his family moved to the safety of Blair House, a century-old historic townhouse nearby on Pennsylvania Avenue.

SAME OLD DILEMMA

Once again, a president was confronted with the question of what to do about the decaying, outdated building. This time renovation was not an option. The structural damage was so widespread that there was no practical way to repair it. The president had only three choices: He could yield to the old suggestion of turning the White House into a historical museum, and build a new President's House in a better location; he could have the old structure torn down and a replica of the old building erected on the same spot; or he could gut the entire building, preserving and reinforcing the original exterior walls.

Truman was not the ardent defender of historical landmarks that Theodore Roosevelt had been. In 1947 he had decided that he wanted a balcony added to the north portico to provide shade for the Blue Room. Despite the strenuous objections of architects and historians, he had gone ahead with his plan. Most experts thought this change, the most drastic to the exterior in over a century, marred the overall appearance of the building.

In this case, however, the weight of tradition moved Truman to follow Roosevelt's lead in preserving at least the outer shell of the grand old structure. The engineers and architects were asked to rebuild a structurally sound new house within the ancient whitewashed walls of the old house. Still irritated by the criticism of his balcony, Truman insisted on taking charge of the project himself. As before, he ignored the advice of experts when it conflicted with his own views.

BLAIR HOUSE

Blair House was the last in a series of distinguished houses that have served as an emergency alternative residence for the president. The four-story brick home stood across the street from the White House, and was nearly as old as its more famous neighbor. It was originally built in 1818 for Dr. Joseph Lovell, who had recently been appointed the first surgeon general of the federal army.

Blair House, the alternate presidential home.

Following Lovell's death in 1836, it was sold to Francis Blair, editor of the nation's foremost pro–Andrew Jackson newspaper. Known as Blair House from that time on, it stayed in the family for more than a century. Among its most distinguished occupants was Francis's son, Montgomery, who served in Abraham Lincoln's cabinet. Lincoln, in fact, frequently strolled across the street to meet with Blair, one of the few in his cabinet whom he completely trusted. Montgomery's son, Gist, eventually came into ownership of the house.

Because of its proximity to the White House, the federal government eagerly bought the property when it became available upon Gist's death in 1942. The purchase proved especially useful when Franklin Roosevelt died while in office in 1944. Not wanting to immediately evict the grieving Eleanor Roosevelt, Harry Truman was able to use Blair House as a temporary residence in the first weeks of his presidency, within easy walking distance of his offices at the White House. When the deteriorated state of the White House forced the Trumans to move out of that building, Blair House again served as a convenient alternative.

TAKING APART THE OLD

The first thing the construction crew had to do was to dismantle and preserve anything from the interior that supervisors wanted saved. The most valuable and beautiful fixtures, paneling, molding, and other woodwork were carefully removed. Each piece was numbered so that it could be returned to its correct position in the rebuilt house, and then put in storage. Everything else of any value was hauled away and sold at auction.

The rest was demolished. A fleet of trucks worked day and night for more than three weeks carting away the wreckage of the old floors, walls, and roof. Even the foundation had to be dug up—the six-foot-deep base that James Hoban had dug for the building was entirely inadequate to anchor the imposing structure of steel and concrete that would replace the old wooden and brick supports. Upon the new foundation, workers constructed a new inner frame of steel, reinforced by concrete, just inside the old walls.

PUTTING IN THE NEW

At first the project advanced as smoothly as Roosevelt's lightning remodeling job. The steel frame was finished by the end of 1950. But the United States soon became heavily involved in the Korean War. Not only did this divert Truman's attention from the White House, but it made an economic impact on the project. With industries churning out materials and supplies for the war

Under Truman's renovations, the outer walls were left intact, a new foundation was laid, and a new steel and concrete inner frame was constructed.

effort, the cost of these items for domestic use escalated. Then, in 1951, the plasterers went on strike.

As the project stalled, project supervisors had to cut some corners. Among the shortcuts was using machine-pressed wood rather than painstakingly reinstalling the old pieces and creating exact replicas by hand to replace damaged ones. Only the State Dining Room was reassembled using the old trim and furnishings.

The Trumans moved back into the White House early in 1952. On March 27, 1952, the president invited television cameras into the place to show the American public the improvements that had

JACQUELINE KENNEDY'S INFLUENCE

No president's wife since Dolley Madison captured the admiration of the public more than "Jackie," as she was known in the press. Not only was she a glamorous woman, but she combined an impeccable taste in decorating with a reverence for history.

Mrs. Kennedy believed that the interior decorating of the White House should reflect the history of each room. To accomplish this, she acquired early-nineteenth-century furniture and paintings and placed them in the public rooms. She also put on display pieces from a priceless gold collection that had been locked away in storage. The effect of her decorating changes in 1961 impressed White House observers. According to one, quoted in *U.S. News & World Report*, "Nothing quite so dramatic has happened to the White House since the British came to town and burned it." Jackie Kennedy's concern was the primary force behind the historical preservation legislation passed in 1961.

Furthermore, Kennedy helped renew public interest in preserving the history of the White House by inviting television cameras in for a tour. Although Truman had done something similar following the reconstruction in the 1950s, Mrs. Kennedy proved a far more charming hostess.

President John F. Kennedy and First Lady Jackie Kennedy.

Included in her tour was a fascinating store of historical anecdotes about each room.

been wrought. Many observers regarded the results as a mixed blessing. On one hand, the White House had been so strengthened that its future was no longer in doubt. With the solid foundation and steel-and-concrete structure now in place, the building should remain safe and sound for hundreds of years. The house was thoroughly modernized and fireproofed, and the jerry-rigged patchwork holes for wiring and pipes replaced. Furthermore, the redigging of the foundation had gouged out space for two new basement levels. This nearly doubled the number of rooms in the building, from 65 to 132. And finally, in most respects, it looked very much like the historic building it had replaced, including the traditional main building floor plan.

Harry Truman completed his reconstruction in 1952.

On the other hand, many valuable furnishings were thrown out and much of the replacement woodwork was not faithful to the original. Critics blasted the entire effort for its lack of attention to architectural history. In the opinion of Ryan and Guiness, "the rebuilding was the greatest calamity to befall the President's House since the fire of 1814."[30]

HISTORICAL PRESERVATION

Since the Truman reconstruction, no significant changes have been made to the structure of the White House. Steps have been taken, however, to make sure that no controversy over such matters as the discarding of historical objects or the addition of features such as the balcony, both of which took place in Truman's administration, would occur again. In 1961, Congress passed a law that protected "the character of the public rooms and the historical objects in the White House collection."[31] Three years later, during the Lyndon Johnson administration, legislation was passed requiring that any proposed changes in the White House be reviewed by the Committee for the Preservation of the White House, whose members were appointed by the president.

That policy remains in force today. Even when Ronald Reagan took the unprecedented step of raising private funds for improvements in the White House, those funds could not be spent without prior approval from the committee.

7

Evolution of a Modern Residence

The original President's House was built at a time when houses had no running water, indoor plumbing, or even closets. Horses were the predominant means of transportation. The invention of electricity, telephones, and air conditioning lay far in the future. Over the course of two centuries, the White House has seen almost constant change as engineers continually tried to install the conveniences and safety features of a modern residence in an old, outdated building.

Heat

With its many large windows and high ceilings, the President's House was a challenge to heat from the day John Adams first stepped into it. James Hoban tried to provide comfortable heating by including thirty-nine fireplaces in the original building. But even that number proved woefully inadequate. The log-burning fireplaces of the time were so inefficient that those close to the fire would roast while people on the other side of the room froze.

Latrobe made several attempts to remedy the problem. In 1804 some of the fireplaces were adapted to the use of coal, a more even-burning fuel. He then took the bold step of installing a revolutionary hot air furnace, recently patented by Daniel Pettibone, in the dining room. The system must not have been satisfactory because, following the 1814 fire, it was not replaced.

Back in charge of operations, Hoban reverted to his plan of trying to overwhelm the problem by sheer force of numbers. In 1817 he added twelve new fireplaces to those already in existence. Nevertheless, presidents and their families continued to complain. Andrew Jackson groused that hell itself could not heat the northwest corner of the building. In Martin Van Buren's administration, the rooms of the main floor were converted to a central coal-fired heating system that circulated hot air. A fireman had to be on duty twenty-four hours a day during the winter months to keep the system going.

In 1845, Millard Fillmore installed a more efficient central heating system that could service twelve rooms. A few years later, Franklin Pierce converted to a hot-water heating system that used less coal and provided more uniform heat to the twelve rooms it served. The renovations of Roosevelt and Truman brought the heating systems up to contemporary standards.

LIGHT

The original President's House was lit by nothing but sunlight, wax candles, and oil lamps. Presidents made do with this until 1848, when gas lighting became popular. The Washington Gas Light Company hooked up the White House to its supply line, and gaslight chandeliers were installed. Sarah Polk had grave suspicions about the reliability of this new form of interior lighting. At her insistence, one of the candlelit chandeliers was retained. The wisdom of her backup plan was proven when the gas lights malfunctioned and went out at the first reception for which they were used.

The Benjamin Harrison family was even more leery of the newfangled electrical outlets that were installed in the White House during the 1880s. The president was so scared of the power of electricity that he usually let the lights in his bedroom burn all night rather than risk shock by turning them off.

WATER

The original President's House relied on well pumps and rainwater collection for usable water, and an outhouse in the back. Hoban proposed a system for running water as early as 1816, but his plans were turned down. When Andrew

Originally, fireplaces were the only means of heating the White House.

Jackson came to the house, servants were still hauling water up from a well in the breezeway or collecting it from pumps that pushed water into the house through open troughs.

In 1833, Jackson had a network of hollow troughs and underground pipes made of hollowed tree trunks installed. In the late 1840s, Fillmore installed what was then becoming the standard method of water distribution—iron pipes. In 1853, Franklin Pierce purchased the residence's first stationary bathtub, complete with a copper water heater. Again, improvements during Theodore Roosevelt's and Truman's administrations brought the plumbing up to modern standards.

COOLING

The cavernous rooms of the President's House generally made the place cooler than most buildings. But Washington's hot, humid summers could be intolerable, and many efforts were made to cool the building. One of the most ambitious came about in Taft's administration. His attempt at a central air conditioning system relied on fans blowing over ice bins in the attic. It never worked well.

The first effective air conditioning system came in with Herbert Hoover in the 1930s. This was extensively modernized in Truman's reconstruction. As for the cooling of food and drink, the refrigerator made its first appearance at the White House in 1845.

TRANSPORTATION

In the early years, the only access to the President's House was via a long, rutted driveway. Traffic going in and out was by foot or horse. James Monroe apparently was the first president who took seriously transportation concerns. Pennsylvania Avenue, leading to the President's House and grounds, was cut during his administration, and he had a stable added onto the west wing.

President William Taft and his wife in a horse-drawn carriage.

For nearly one hundred years, presidents who had to travel any distance from their home rode in a fancy horse-drawn carriage. Not until the 1910s was automobile development advanced to the point that William Taft ordered a fleet of cars to replace the traditional presidential horsedrawn carriages. Dwight Eisenhower ushered in another new era in transportation when he had helicopters land on the White House lawn.

OTHER WHITE HOUSE OCCUPANTS

Throughout much of its history, the White House has been home to creatures other than humans. Not all of these animals were of the small, housebroken variety. Thomas Jefferson had perhaps the most unusual pets: grizzly bears, a species previously unknown to Europeans, that had been brought back from the Lewis and Clark expedition and were kept on the grounds in cages.

Sheep roam the White House lawn.

While many presidents were fond of horses, Ulysses Grant probably spent more time in the White House stables than any other. Keeping cows on the property for milk and butter was a common practice that did not end until Woodrow Wilson's administration in the 1910s. Wilson, however, substituted sheep during World War I as an economical way of keeping the lawn trimmed and to provide wool.

As for smaller pets, dogs and cats have been common guests at the presidential mansion. Lyndon Johnson's beagles and George Bush's dog, Millie, were some of the more notable canines. Caroline Kennedy, John Kennedy's daughter, kept hamsters, who occasionally escaped from their cage and caused a massive hunt throughout the house.

No pets, however, had a greater impact on the White House than the pigeons kept by Tad Lincoln in the 1860s. According to one frustrated White House worker, quoted by Seale in *The White House: An American Idea*, "Twenty years later the caretakers of the Treasury and other public buildings were still striving to exterminate the hardy survivors of Tad's breeding."

ENTERTAINMENT

The early presidents lived at a time when in-home entertainment consisted mainly of receptions, parties, and recitals. Even in the early 1800s, much of the American public looked with disapproval on entertainment, considering it frivolous and unproductive. John Quincy Adams ran into such a storm of criticism in the 1820s when

The White House's outdoor pool, added by Gerald Ford. The first pool was built in the 1930s for Franklin D. Roosevelt.

he purchased a billiard table for the President's House that he was forced to pay for it out of his own funds. Attitudes had changed enough by the 1870s, however, to allow Ulysses Grant to make the billiard room his most cherished part of the house. By the turn of the twenty-first century, Bill Clinton could watch first-run movies in his own private theater in the White House without public outcry.

A different type of diversion has been the focus of a seesaw battle between presidents. The first White House swimming pool was built in the 1930s through a private fundraising effort by people concerned that Franklin Roosevelt, who could not walk unaided after he contracted polio, needed a place to exercise. Richard Nixon, however, was not particularly concerned with exercise. In the 1970s he ordered the pool boarded over and replaced by a press room. No sooner did Nixon resign from office than fitness enthusiast Gerald Ford put in a new pool, this one outdoors.

HEALTH CONCERNS

The White House was not designed to meet modern health standards. In fact, throughout much of its history, it had a reputation as an unhealthy and possibly deadly place to live. Part of the problem was its location, just above a large, rather stagnant marsh. Many early presidents, including Thomas Jefferson, believed that swamps gave off poisonous gases that caused disease. These fears increased in the late 1840s when James Polk died soon upon leaving office and Zachary Taylor died shortly after taking the oath. Fear of disease from the swamp, along with the irritating mosquitoes it harbored, caused many presidents to leave the White House during the summer months as a health precaution. The marsh gradually dried up and filled in over the years, but it was considered a health hazard as late as the 1870s.

In the view of some presidents, the house itself was a breeding ground for sickness. Beginning with John Adams, they complained of the dampness and mildew. Abraham Lincoln once said that the ground-level rooms reminded him "of old country taverns, if not something you have smelled on the edge of some swamp."[32]

One of the most persistent health problems associated with the President's House has been rats and mice. In Jefferson's time, most people thought these vermin came from the stables. But their efforts to seal off the house from the pests failed, as did all efforts to cope with the problem for the next eighty years.

During Benjamin Harrison's administration, experts believed they could solve the problem by tearing up and renovating the basement, where most of the creatures lived and bred. They were wrong.

Similar hopes that the reconstruction during Theodore Roosevelt's term would clear out the mice met with even worse disappointment. The rodents seemed to be more populous than ever. At one point, Roosevelt's staff hired a man who specialized in rodent removal. He brought in ferrets and dogs and set them loose about the building for two nights. This brought only temporary relief. After a while, White House residents became resigned to the situation. When the Trumans moved into the White House in the late 1940s, Eleanor Roosevelt matter-of-factly commented that they should not be surprised to see mice on the draperies and scurrying across the railings during receptions. Again, when Harry Truman had the entire building gutted and rebuilt almost from scratch in the 1950s, the rodent problem finally abated, although some problems persisted into the 1970s.

The greatest health hazard associated with houses when the President's Mansion was built was fire. On that count, the building has been extremely fortunate to have survived in its present state. Not counting the purposeful burning by the British, only two minor fires have occurred on the premises. On January 17, 1867, fire broke out in the greenhouse, and on December 25, 1929, a fire caused considerable damage in the executive offices.

MAKING THE WHITE HOUSE SAFE

Over the decades, the strongest argument in favor of moving the president's residence to a different building has been the safety of the president and his family. The White House was not constructed to shield the president from the high-tech tools of modern terrorists and assassins.

The safety of the house has been a concern ever since a wave of political assassinations swept Europe in the 1820s. At that time, however, the President's House was still in a fairly isolated location. James Monroe was able to establish a secure building simply by stationing sharpshooters on the roof. Bars have guarded basement windows since the 1820s. As the city of Washington grew more congested, however, people became more concerned about keeping disgruntled and unhinged people away from the president. John Tyler established the Metropolitan Police for his protection. A decade later, in the 1850s, Franklin Pierce took the further step of hiring a personal bodyguard.

ERA OF ASSASSINATIONS

No president has lived in greater peril in the White House than Abraham Lincoln. Washington, D.C., was in the middle of slave country, and so was extremely hostile to Lincoln, who had spoken forcefully against slavery when he arrived to take office. Incredibly, no federal troops were available to protect the president in his first days. A group of rugged Kansans, armed with muskets, voluntarily set up a patrol of the White House until the troops arrived.

In July 1861, the U.S. Army was defeated at Bull Run in the first major battle of the Civil War. The federal troops fled and scattered, leaving the road to Washington wide open. Lincoln lay on his couch at night, unable to sleep, while Confederate campfires burned near the outskirts of the capital. The Confederates, however, failed to follow up their victory with an attack on Washington.

The last half of the nineteenth century was a deadly time for U.S. presidents. Three of them—Lincoln, Garfield, and McKinley—fell to assassins' bullets, although none of the assassinations took place at the White House. The McKinley assassination led to the formation of the Secret Service in 1906. Since that time, Secret Service agents have taken up posts at the White House to protect the president from harm. In the 1930s, Herbert Hoover began the practice of stationing permanent Secret Service guards at both entrances to the Oval Office.

ASSAULTS ON THE WHITE HOUSE

While attacks on the president have been alarmingly frequent in U.S. history, no one has been able to harm the president in the confines of the White House. There have, however, been a number of attempts over the years, most of them inept. The first recorded attack was in the 1840s when a drunken painter threw rocks at John Tyler on the south lawn.

A more serious incident occurred early in Andrew Johnson's term. White House personnel engaged in a shootout with a gunman trying to assassinate the new president. Johnson, however, was never in any danger during the encounter.

Despite fears about its lack of security, the White House remained free from attack until recent times. The most bizarre attacks have come from the air. In 1974 a disturbed U.S. army private hovered over the White House in a plane. He was shot down and captured on the south lawn before he could do any damage. In September 1994, a suicidal man stole a single-engine plane from an airport north of Baltimore. Somehow evading radar detection, he came in low over the White House at 2 A.M., and nicked a hedge. The plane skidded out of control over the lawn and smashed into the White House two stories beneath the bedroom where Bill Clinton slept. The pilot died instantly, but no one else was hurt and the damage to the building was minimal.

Clinton survived a rash of armed attacks on the White House. In October 1994, a man fired twenty-seven rounds of ammunition from a semiautomatic assault weapon into the White House. Two months later, another attacker fired four bullets into the building. In both cases, bulletproof glass installed at the White House prevented any real danger to the occupants.

TIGHTENING THE RING OF SECURITY

During the twentieth century, advancements in weaponry, explosives, and transportation made the world a more dangerous place. The White House has been adapted to protect against those dangers. Prior to World War II, the White House grounds were easily accessible. The only barrier was a three-foot-high fence that existed mainly to keep out dogs. No security forces were stationed outside the doors of the White House. Following the Japanese attack on Pearl Harbor in 1941, however, officials moved guards from the building out to the fence. A small street that came within two hundred feet of the Oval Office on the west side was closed. Safety inspectors from the army gave the White House a thorough evaluation and found it vulnerable to the kind of air attack that destroyed the U.S. naval base at Pearl Harbor. They suggested such radical measures as painting the White House so that it would blend into the surroundings and be difficult to spot. Franklin Roosevelt flatly refused the suggestion, but he agreed to a number of lesser measures such as storing gas masks in the house, installing blackout curtains on the windows, and canceling public tours. At first he resisted the idea of constructing an underground air raid shelter, but he finally gave in. During the 1950s, an improved, bombproof room beneath the basement was constructed for Dwight Eisenhower.

ANTITERRORISM MEASURES

In the last half of the twentieth century, security officials took extra precautions whenever danger threatened. During the tumultuous days of the Vietnam War and civil rights protests in the 1960s, the usual contingent of Secret Service agents protecting Lyndon Johnson was reinforced by armed soldiers. In response to car bombings in trouble spots around the world, concrete posts were set up on the Pennsylvania Avenue sidewalk in front of the White House to prevent any vehicle from driving across the lawn. In the late 1980s, bulletproof glass was installed as a precaution against long-range sniping.

During the Gulf War in the early 1990s, White House tours were again suspended for brief periods. Air defense teams patrolled the top floor of the building with rifles, and ground-to-air missile squads were put on alert at the nearby National Airport. On May 20, 1995, following the devastating bombing of a federal building in Oklahoma City, federal officials took the drastic step of permanently closing Pennsylvania Avenue and rerouting its traffic of twenty-six thousand vehicles per day.

For security reasons, the building plan of the White House is kept top secret. The exact location of such safety features as a tunnel under the Oval Office leading to the basement of the family quarters is never disclosed. Such precautionary adaptations are among the many ways in which an eighteenth-century building has been adapted to the world of the twentieth century.

Epilogue

Many times over the course of the nation's history, plans have been made to build a new home for the president. But in the end, tradition has always won out. Despite years of controversy and debate triggered by the building's unique function as both a national shrine and a private residence, the White House remains as one of the few great landmarks of the nation's founding that has not been relegated to some substitute use.

The White House endures not because of any remarkable design or construction but because it reflects the nation's journey through time. Every president has brought to the White House his own ideas about how the place should be decorated and remodeled. Some of these changes live on through the decades; others disappear during the renovation that takes place after each president's term ends.

The mystique of the White House comes from its position at center stage during the nation's most critical moments. It was in the White House that Thomas Jefferson hatched the plan to

The White House remains a symbol of American tradition while adapting to the contemporary needs of the country.

send one of his secretaries, Meriwether Lewis, out west on the Lewis and Clark expedition that opened the nation's eyes to its vast resources. It was in the dark halls of the White House that Abraham Lincoln paced on many a sleepless night as he tried to hold the country together in the face of a brutal civil war. It was in the East Room of the White House that silent crowds mourned a murdered president as they passed by the casket bearing John Kennedy's body.

Today, it is more solidly entrenched than ever in its traditional roles. With a staff of 115 to maintain its 132 rooms, the White House provides an elegant home for the presidential family, a stately setting for the 40,000 guests who are hosted there annually, and a fascinating destination for the 1.5 million tourists who enter its doors each year.

NOTES

Introduction

1. Kenneth W. Leish, *The White House*. New York: Newsweek, 1972, p. 1.
2. Quoted in Leish, *The White House*, p. 67.
3. Quoted in Carl Sandburg, *Abraham Lincoln: The War Years*, vol. 1. New York: Harcourt Brace, 1939, pp. 137–38.
4. Quoted in *The White House: An Historic Guide*. Washington, DC: White House Historical Association, 1982, p. 61.

Chapter 1: The Federal City

5. Quoted in Daniel D. Reiff, *Washington Architecture: 1791–1861*. Washington, DC: U.S. Commission of Fine Arts, 1971, p. 2.
6. William Seale, *The White House: An American Idea*. Washington, DC: American Institute of Architecture, 1992, p. 1.
7. Reiff, *Washington Architecture*, p. 11.

Chapter 2: Designing the President's House

8. Quoted in William Ryan and Desmond Guiness, *The White House: An Architectural History*. New York: McGraw-Hill, 1980, p. 181.
9. Quoted in Seale, *The White House*, p. 5.
10. Quoted in Marshall B. Davidson, *The American Heritage History of Notable American Houses*. New York: American Heritage, 1971, p. 132.
11. Quoted in *The White House: An Historic Guide*, p. 106.
12. Quoted in Leish, *The White House*, p. 21.
13. Quoted in Ryan and Guiness, *The White House*, p. 34.
14. Ryan and Guiness, *The White House*, p. 70.
15. Quoted in Davidson, *The American Heritage History of Notable American Houses*, p. 125.

Chapter 3: Building the President's House

16. Quoted in Lee H. Nelson, *White House Stone Carving*. Washington, DC: U.S. Department of the Interior, 1992, p. 4.
17. Nelson, *White House Stone Carving*, p. 4.
18. Nelson, *White House Stone Carving*, p. 8.
19. Seale, *The White House*, p. 32.
20. Quoted in Ryan and Guiness, *The White House*, p. 122.

Chapter 4: Fire and Rebuilding

21. Quoted in Ryan and Guiness, *The White House*, p. 112.

22. Quoted in Leish, *The White House*, p. 26.

23. Seale, *The White House*, p. 69.

Chapter 5: Renovations: The First Century

24. Quoted in Leish, *The White House*, p. 40.

25. Ryan and Guiness, *The White House*, p. 132.

26. Quoted in *The White House: An Historic Guide*, p. 131.

Chapter 6: Renovations: The Second Century

27. Quoted in William Seale, *The President's House*, vol. 2. Washington, DC: White House Historical Association, 1986, p. 657.

28. Seale, *The White House*, p. 201.

29. Quoted in Leish, *The White House*, p. 145.

30. Ryan and Guiness, *The White House*, p. 132.

31. Quoted in "A Glimpse of Life in Today's White House," *U.S. News & World Report*, April 3, 1961, p. 66.

Chapter 7: Evolution of a Modern Residence

32. Quoted in *The White House: An Historic Guide*, p. 12.

FOR FURTHER READING

Marlene Targ Brill, *Building the Capital City*. New York: Childrens Press, 1996. A very easy-to-read but nonetheless informative book on how Washington, DC, including its great buildings such as the White House, was built.

Judith St. George, *The White House: Cornerstone of a Nation*. New York: Putnam, 1990. The most detailed and informative book for young readers on the subject of the White House.

R. Conrad Stein, *Washington, DC*. New York: Childrens Press, 1999. The most up-to-date book on the subject is packed with photographs and information on the nation's capital, including material on the origins of federal buildings such as the White House.

Kate Walters, *The White House*. New York: Scholastic, 1991. Primarily a photoessay, this book includes fascinating portraits of key White House figures.

WORKS CONSULTED

"A Glimpse of Life in Today's White House," *U.S. News & World Report,* April 3, 1961.

Blair House: Past and Present. Washington, DC: U.S. Department of State, 1945. This slim book relates the history of the Blair House, where Truman lived during much of his presidency.

Marshall B. Davidson, *The American Heritage History of Notable American Houses.* New York: American Heritage, 1971. This architectural anthology includes a section on the White House as well as anecdotes about the architectural undertakings of Washington and Jefferson.

Joan Paterson Kerr, *A Bully Father.* New York: Random House, 1995. Included in this affectionate look at Theodore Roosevelt are tales of White House mischief by the White House Gang.

Kenneth W. Leish, *The White House.* New York: Newsweek, 1972. A thorough examination of the history of the White House from the country's founding to the presidency of Richard Nixon.

Lee H. Nelson, *White House Stone Carving,* Washington, DC: U.S. Department of the Interior, 1992. The book presents the little-known story of the craftsmen responsible for the ornate carvings in the White House.

Daniel D. Reiff, *Washington Architecture: 1791–1861.* Washington, DC: U.S. Commission of Fine Arts, 1971. This more scholarly book includes a section on the construction of the White House.

William Ryan and Desmond Guiness, *The White House: An Architectural History.* New York: McGraw-Hill, 1980. Along with Leish and Seale, these authors present a fairly complete view of the history of the White House, from the viewpoint of architectural critics.

Carl Sandburg, *Abraham Lincoln: The War Years,* vol. 1. New York: Harcourt Brace, 1939. This volume of Sandburg's classic biography includes details about the president's life in the White House.

William Seale, *The President's House,* vols.1 and 2. Washington, DC: White House Historical Association, 1986. The most detailed examination of the White House and those who shaped and lived in it, from a historical and biographical point of view.

William Seale, *The White House: An American Idea.* Washington, DC: American Institute of Architecture, 1992. A condensed version of Seale's earlier works, with more photographs.

Hugh Sidey, "Never Safe Enough," *Time,* November 14, 1994.

The White House: An Historic Guide. Washington, DC: White House Historical Association, 1982. A brief and informal telling of the two centuries of the White House.

INDEX

PICTURE CREDITS

Cover photos: White House Historical Association (left); PhotoDisk, Vol. 25, Government and Social Issues (top right); White House Historical Association/National Park Service (bottom right)

©Bettmann/Corbis, 23, 26, 74

©Corbis, 8, 9, 45

Hayward and Blanche Cirker, *Dictionary of American Portraits*, Dover publications, Inc., 1967, 59

Library of Congress, 11, 12, 19, 28, 36, 37, 43, 44, 47, 48, 49, 52, 53, 54, 57, 58, 60, 61, 62, 64, 67, 68, 69, 72, 75, 77, 78, 79, 80, 85

Maryland Historical Society, 29

National Archives, 16

Martha Schierholz, 21

Prints Old and Rare, 41

White House Historical Association, 20, 33, 39

White House Historical Association/National Park Service, 73

ABOUT THE AUTHOR

Nathan Aaseng is the author of more than 140 books for young readers on a wide variety of subjects. More than three dozen of his works have won awards. A former microbiologist with degrees in biology and English from Luther College (Iowa), he currently lives in Eau Claire, Wisconsin, with his wife and four children.

Henry County Library System
Locust Grove Public Library
P.O. Box 240, 3918 Highway 42
Locust Grove, GA 30248